Lecture Notes in Computer Science 14246

The series Lecture Notes in Computer Science (LNCS), including its subseries Lecture Notes in Artificial Intelligence (LNAI) and Lecture Notes in Bioinformatics (LNBI), has established itself as a medium for the publication of new developments in computer science and information technology research, teaching, and education.

LNCS enjoys close cooperation with the computer science R & D community, the series counts many renowned academics among its volume editors and paper authors, and collaborates with prestigious societies. Its mission is to serve this international community by providing an invaluable service, mainly focused on the publication of conference and workshop proceedings and postproceedings. LNCS commenced publication in 1973.

Daphna Link-Sourani · Esra Abaci Turk ·
Christopher Macgowan · Jana Hutter ·
Andrew Melbourne · Roxane Licandro
Editors

Perinatal, Preterm and Paediatric Image Analysis

8th International Workshop, PIPPI 2023
Held in Conjunction with MICCAI 2023
Vancouver, BC, Canada, October 12, 2023
Proceedings

Editors
Daphna Link-Sourani 📵
Technion – Israel Institute of Technology
Haifa, Israel

Christopher Macgowan 📵
The Hospital For Sick Children Research
Toronto, ON, Canada

Andrew Melbourne 📵
King's College London
London, UK

Esra Abaci Turk 📵
Boston Children's Hospital
Boston, MA, USA

Jana Hutter 📵
King's College London
School of Biomedical Engineering
and Imaging Sciences
London, UK

Friedrich-Alexander Universität, MR-Physik
am Universitätsklinikum Erlangen
Erlangen, Germany

Roxane Licandro 📵
Medical University of Vienna
Department of Biomedical Imaging
Vienna, Austria

Image-guided Therapy
Computational Image Research
Vienna, Austria

ISSN 0302-9743   ISSN 1611-3349 (electronic)
Lecture Notes in Computer Science
ISBN 978-3-031-45543-8   ISBN 978-3-031-45544-5 (eBook)
https://doi.org/10.1007/978-3-031-45544-5

This Springer imprint is published by the registered company Springer Nature Switzerland AG
The registered company address is: Gewerbestrasse 11, 6330 Cham, Switzerland

Paper in this product is recyclable.

Preface

The application of advanced imaging and analysis techniques to fetal, neonatal, and paediatric imaging is of interest to a substantial proportion of the MICCAI (Medical Image Computing and Computer-Assisted Intervention) community. Advanced medical image analysis allows the detailed scientific study of conditions such as prematurity, placental and fetal development in singleton and multiple pregnancies, in addition to conditions unique to the period from early childhood to adolescence and the lifelong consequences of such diseases. The goal of the Perinatal, Preterm and Paediatric Image Analysis (PIPPI) workshop is to provide a focused platform for the researchers in the MICCAI community to discuss the challenges of image analysis techniques as applied to the fetal and infant settings.

This year's workshop took place on October 12, 2023, as a satellite event of the 26th International Conference on Medical Image Computing and Computer Assisted Intervention (MICCAI 2023). Our keynote speaker – Dafna Ben Bashat (Tel Aviv Sourasky Medical Center, Israel) - was invited to PIPPI 2023 to stimulate discussions, present recent research, and highlight future challenges in this field. Following our experience from the workshop in 2022, PIPPI 2023 made use of a hybrid setup, allowing participants to join either in person or online. In PIPPI 2023, we modified the PIPPI CIRCLE session as a small group discussion. Each group comprised scientists from clinics, industry, and academia and formed break-out discussion sessions, followed by a plenary discussion based on the outcome of each group discussion in the break-out session.

For the first time, this year PIPPI 2023 was endorsed by FIT'NG (Fetal, Infant, Toddler Neuroimaging Group)[1] with a tailored best poster award to honor outstanding PIPPI 2023 contributions in the fetal neuroimaging field. Also a PIPPI best paper prize was awarded to the best publication (Winners are listed on the workshop webpage[2]).

PIPPI 2023 received original, innovative, and mathematically rigorous papers related to the analysis of fetal and infant imaging data. The methods presented in these proceedings cover the full scope of medical image analysis, including segmentation, registration, classification, reconstruction, population analysis, and advanced structural, functional, and longitudinal modeling, all with an application to younger cohorts. All papers were subjected to a rigorous double-blind review process, involving evaluation by two expert reviewers from the Program Committee. 71% of the papers were accepted for publication, 5 papers were selected for oral presentation and 5 papers were selected for poster presentation at PIPPI 2023 alongside four late-breaking short abstracts.

---

[1] www.fitng.org

[2] https://pippiworkshop.github.io/

We would like to thank everyone who helped to make this year's workshop a success.

October 2023

Andrew Melbourne
Christopher Macgowan
Daphna Link-Sourani
Esra Abaci Turk
Jana Hutter
Roxane Licandro

Organization

Program Committee Chairs

Andrew Melbourne	King's College London, UK
Christopher Macgowan	University of Toronto, Canada
Daphna Link-Sourani	Technion - Israel Institute of Technology, Israel
Esra Abaci Turk	Boston Children's Hospital, Harvard Medical School, USA
Jana Hutter	King's College London, School of Biomedical Engineering and Imaging Sciences, UK and Friedrich-Alexander Universität, MR-Physik am Universitätsklinikum Erlangen, Germany
Roxane Licandro	Medical University of Vienna, Department of Biomedical Imaging, Austria and Image-guided Therapy, Computational Image Research, Austria

Program Committee

Ai Wern Chung	Boston Children's Hospital, USA
Alicia Dagle	Columbia University, USA
Athena Taymourtash	Medical University of Vienna, Austria
Bianca Burger	Medical University of Vienna, Austria
Celine Steger	University of Zurich, Switzerland
Christoph Fürböck	Medical University of Vienna
Christopher Roy	Lausanne University Hospital, Switzerland
Hongwei Li	Technical University of Munich, Germany, University of Zurich, Switzerland
Jeffrey N. Stout	Boston Children's Hospital, USA
Jorge Perez-Gonzalez	Universidad Nacional Autónoma de México, Mexico
Junshen Xu	Massachusetts Institute of Technology, USA
Lilla Zöllei	Massachusetts General Hospital, USA
Liu Li	Imperial College London, UK
Maik Dannecker	Technical University of Munich, Germany
Sara Neves Silvia	King's College London, UK
Tamaz Amiranashvili	University of Zurich, Switzerland

Veronika Zimmer   Technical University Munich, Germany
Yael Zaffrani-Reznikov   Technion - Israel Institute of Technology, Israel
Zhenglun Alan Wei   Worcester Polytechnic Institute, USA

Contents

Placental and Cervical Image Analysis

Infant Video Analysis

Fetal Brain Image Analysis

FetMRQC: Automated Quality Control for Fetal Brain MRI

Thomas Sanchez[1,2(✉)], Oscar Esteban[1], Yvan Gomez[3,5],
Elisenda Eixarch[3,4], and Meritxell Bach Cuadra[1,2]

[1] Department of Radiology, Lausanne University Hospital (CHUV) and University of
Lausanne (UNIL), Lausanne, Switzerland
thomas.sanchez@unil.ch
[2] CIBM Center for Biomedical Imaging, Lausanne, Switzerland
[3] BCNatal Fetal Medicine Research Center (Hospital Clínic and Hospital Sant Joan
de Déu), Universitat de Barcelona, Barcelona, Spain
[4] IDIBAPS and CIBERER, Barcelona, Spain
[5] Department Woman-Mother-Child, CHUV, Lausanne, Switzerland

Abstract. Quality control (QC) has long been considered essential to
guarantee the reliability of neuroimaging studies. It is particularly important for fetal brain MRI, where large and unpredictable fetal motion can
lead to substantial artifacts in the acquired images. Existing methods
for fetal brain quality assessment operate at the *slice* level, and fail to
get a comprehensive picture of the quality of an image, that can only be
achieved by looking at the *entire* brain volume. In this work, we propose
FetMRQC, a machine learning framework for automated image quality
assessment tailored to fetal brain MRI, which extracts an ensemble of
quality metrics that are then used to predict experts' ratings. Based
on the manual ratings of more than 1000 low-resolution stacks acquired
across two different institutions, we show that, compared with existing quality metrics, FetMRQC is able to generalize out-of-domain, while
being interpretable and data efficient. We also release a novel manual
quality rating tool designed to facilitate and optimize quality rating of
fetal brain images.

Our tool, along with all the code to generate, train and evaluate
the model is available at https://github.com/Medical-Image-Analysis-
Laboratory/fetal_brain_qc/.

Keywords: Image quality assessment · Fetal brain MRI

TS is supported by the Era-net Neuron MULTIFACT project (SNSF 31NE30_203977),
OE is supported by the Swiss National Science Foundation (SNSF #185872), the NIMH
(RF1MH12186), and the CZI (EOSS5/'NiPreps'). YG acknowledges support from the
SICPA foundation and EE is supported by the Instituto de Salud Carlos III (ISCIII)
(AC21_2/00016). We acknowledge access to the facilities and expertise of the CIBM
Center for Biomedical Imaging, a Swiss research center of excellence founded and sup-
ported by CHUV, UNIL, EPFL, UNIGE and HUG.

D. Link-Sourani et al. (Eds.): PIPPI 2023, LNCS 14246, pp. 3–16, 2023.
https://doi.org/10.1007/978-3-031-45544-5_1

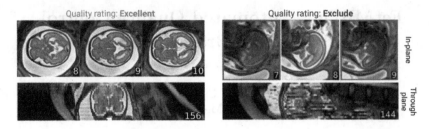

Fig. 1. Examples of clinical image quality: left, excellent quality, and right, low quality. On the **right**, the stack would be excluded from further analysis due to significant intensity changes between many slices and strong signal drop; in the through-plane view, strong inter-slice motion makes it difficult to discern the structure of the brain.

1   Introduction

Magnetic Resonance Imaging (MRI) of the fetal brain is increasingly complementing ultrasound imaging to diagnose abnormalities, thanks to its unmatched soft tissue contrast [1,2]. However, inherent noise sources and imaging artifacts, such as fetal motion, can degrade the quality of the acquired images and jeopardize subsequent analyses. Indeed, insufficient MRI data quality has been shown to bias neuroradiological assessment and statistical analyses [3–5]. Therefore, establishing objective image quality assessment and control (QA/QC) protocols for neuroimaging studies has long been considered critical to ensure their reliability, generalization, and replicability [6,7]. More recently, some QA/QC tools have been popularized for the adult brain and attempt to automate and aid exclusion decisions [8–12]. Unfortunately, these techniques have found generalization across imaging devices extremely challenging [8]. Moreover, they are inapplicable to fetal MRI, as they rely on invalid prior knowledge, e.g., assuming that the head is surrounded by air or the relative position of the brain with respect to the axis of the bore of the scanner. This is true in particular for MRIQC [8], from which this work is inspired.

In fetal brain MRI, QA/QC has been approached implicitly within super-resolution reconstruction (SRR) methods [13–17]. SRR builds a high-resolution, isotropic 3D volume from several differently-oriented, consecutive stacks of 2D slices with substantially lower resolution on the through-plane axis (i.e., anisotropic resolution). Typically, SRR methods rely on a manual selection of stacks that are deemed adequate for reconstruction. These methods may incorporate an automated QC stage for outlier rejection that excludes sub-standard slices or pixels from the input low-resolution stacks [13,14,17,18]. Outside of fetal brain MRI, Uus et al. [19] have explored methods to automate the rejection of poorly registered stacks. However, bad quality series can remain detrimental to the final quality of the reconstruction, even when SRR pipelines include outlier rejection schemes. This is why, in this work, we focus on the QA/QC of low-resolution (LR) stacks.

Recent work has applied deep learning on QA/QC of LR stacks of fetal brain MRI [20–22]. These solutions automatically identify problematic slices for exclusion (QC), and, if streamlined with the acquisition, their short inference time permits re-acquiring corrupted slices [23] (QA). However, not all artifacts can be seen by analyzing single slices. For instance, inter-slice motion (visible on the right of Fig. 1), a strong bias field in the through-plane direction, or an incomplete field of view can often clearly be seen only when considering the entire volume.

We propose FetMRQC, a framework for QA/QC of clinical fetal brain MRI, operating on stacks of LR, T2-weighted (T2w) images. Inspired by MRIQC [8], FetMRQC generates a visual report corresponding to each input stack, for efficient screening and manual QA. The tool also automatically extracts an ensemble of image quality metrics (IQMs) that reflect some quality feature. Finally, we propose a learning framework to automatically predict image quality from the IQMs corresponding to new images. We manually assessed more than 1000 LR stacks acquired across two different institutions and several MRI scanners within each. Using these manual quality annotations, we quantitatively assess FetMRQC in two QA/QC tasks, namely, regression and binary classification (inclusion/exclusion). Our results demonstrate the feasibility of automated QA/QC of T2w images of the fetal brain and the substantial improvement of SRR after QC of subpar stacks.

2 Methodology

FetMRQC comprehends two major elements to implement QA/QC protocols of *unprocessed* (LR stacks) fetal brain MRI data. First, the tool builds upon MRIQC's paradigm and generates an individual QA report for each LR stack to assist and optimize screening and annotation by experts. Second, *FetMRQC* proposes a learning framework (Fig. 3) based on *image quality metrics* (IQMs) extracted from the data to automate the assessment.

2.1 Data

We retrospectively collected LR T2w stacks from 146 subjects retrieved from two existing databases at two different institutions, CHUV and BCNatal. The data were acquired on different Siemens scanners and a common MR scheme (Half fourier Single-shot Turbo spin-Echo; HASTE), at 1.5T and 3T, with both normal and pathological cases. The full list of parameters is detailed in Table 4 in the Appendix. The corresponding local ethics committees independently approved the studies under which data were collected, and all participants gave written informed consent. CHUV provided 61 subjects, with an average of 7.9±3.0 LR stacks per subject. The BCNatal provided 85 subjects, 5.8 ± 3.4 stacks per subject. The aggregate sample size is $N=1010$ LR series.

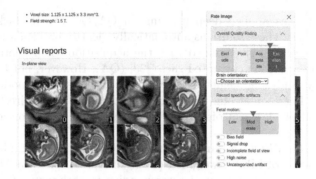

Fig. 2. Visual quality assessment tool proposed in this work. The HTML report gives some general information on the anonymized scan, displays all slices with brain content, as well as both orthogonal through-plane views, as seen on Fig. 1.

2.2 Manual QA of Fetal MRI Stacks

Akin to MRIQC [8], *FetMRQC* generates an HTML-based report adapted to the QA of fetal brains for each input LR stack (Fig. 2). The input dataset is required to comply with the Brain Imaging Data Structure (BIDS) [24], a format widely adopted in the neuroimaging community. The reports are generated using an image with a corresponding brain mask. This mask can be extracted automatically, and in this work, we used MONAIfbs [25]. Each individual-stack report has a QA utility (the so-called *rating widget*, with which raters can fill in an overall quality score, the in-plane orientation, and the presence and grading of artifacts showcased by the stack. We chose also to use an interval (as opposed to categorical) rating scale with four main quality ranges: $[0, 1]$: exclude – $(1, 2]$: poor – $(2, 3]$: acceptable – $(3, 4]$: excellent. Interval ratings simplify statistical modeling, set lower bounds to *annotation noise*, and enable the *inference* task where a continuous quality score is assigned to input images, rather than broad categories.

We generated the individual report corresponding to each of the 1010 LR stacks. Two raters independently annotated each 555 of the dataset using the proposed tool, which yielded 100 stacks annotated by both raters to test inter-rater variability. These 100 stacks were randomly selected. Rater , YG, 1 is a maternal-fetal physician with 5 years of experience in neuroimaging, and Rater 2, MBC, is an engineer with 20 years of experience in neuroimaging.

2.3 IQMs Extraction and Learning

IQMs in Fetal Brain MRI. Leveraging the same workflow that generates the individual reports, a number of IQMs were extracted from the full stack and from the information within the brain mask. Since only a few IQMs defined by MRIQC can be applied to fetal brains, we implemented a set of IQMs specific to the application at hand. In [14], Kainz et al. proposed a `rank_error`

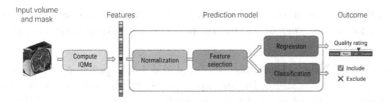

Fig. 3. Proposed automated IQA pipeline. Given an input image and the corresponding brain mask, an ensemble of IQMs are extracted, and then processed in a prediction model. IQMs are normalized and irrelevant entries are removed before being fed into a regression or classification model, that produces the final outcome.

based on the estimated compressibility of an LR stack. Later on, brain mask-derived measures were used such as the volume of the brain mask, `mask_volume`, in [18] or its `centroid` in [26]. Recently, deep learning-based IQM slice-wise and stack-wise have been proposed, `dl_slice_iqa` [21] and `dl_stack_iqa` [27], which respectively do slice-wise and stack wise quality assessment[12].

We propose additional IQMs for quality prediction that have not previously been used in the context of fetal brain MRI. They can roughly be categorized into two groups, and full details are provided in Table 3 in the Appendix. In a nutshell, **intensity-based** IQMs directly rely on the voxel values of the image. These include summary statistics [8] like mean, median, and percentiles. We also re-use metrics traditionally used for outlier rejection [13,14,18] to quantify the intensity difference between slices in a volume. We also compute entropy [8], estimate the level of bias using N4 bias field correction [28] and estimate the sharpness of the image with Laplace and Sobel filters. The second type of metrics are **shape-based** and operate directly on the automatically extracted brain mask. We propose to use a morphological closing to detect through-plane motion, as well as edge detection to estimate the variation of the surface of the brain mask.

Variation on the Metrics. All the IQMs operate on LR images or masks and can be modified by various transformations of the data. For instance, Kainz et al. [14] evaluated their metrics only on the third of the slices closest to the center of a given LR volume. We include various variations on the IQMs, including considering the whole ROI instead of the centermost slices (`_full`). Other variations include keeping or masking the maternal background, aggregating point estimates using mean, median, or other estimators, computing information theoretic metrics on the union or intersection of masks, etc. Finally, `slice_loss` metrics can be either computed as a pairwise comparison between all slices (by default) or only on a window of neighboring slices (`_window`). With all the dif-

---

[1] We use the *pre-trained* models throughout these experiments, as we want to test the off-the-shelf value of these IQMs.

[2] The method of Liao et al. [22] was not included because their code is not publicly available, and we could not get in contact with the authors.

ferent variations, we arrive at a total of 75 different features. See Fig. 7 in the Appendix for a cross-correlation matrix between all IQMs on our dataset.

Feature-Wise Normalization. We explored both global and subject-wise standard and robust scaling. In our experiments, we did not notice substantial changes between global and subject-wise scaling, and for the sake of simplicity, we adopted global scaling in the rest of this work.

Feature-Selection and Dimensionality Reduction. We explored feature variance and correlations. We removed irrelevant features (variance = 0 for a given subset of data) and drop IQMs that are highly correlated with each other (with threshold 0.8 and 0.9). We also removed features which do not contribute more than noise using the Winnow algorithm [29] with extremely randomized trees [8]. Finally, we also explored using principal component analysis to reduce dimensionality and construct orthogonal features as input of the model.

Model Selection and Evaluation Through Nested Cross-Validation. Nested cross-validation (CV) is a fully automated mechanism to perform model selection and evaluation without introducing optimistic biases [30]. In this framework, an outer CV loop benchmarks the expected performance of the family of models represented by the inner loop. An inner CV loop is executed for each fold of the outer loop to select the best-performing model on average.

We set up the nested CV framework with five folds in both the inner and outer loops (80% train, 20% test at each level), for both the regression and classification tasks. We ensured to group together all the LR stacks of each subject to avoid data leaking between the training and testing fold. For the regression task, we evaluated linear regression, gradient boosting, and random forests. For classification, we considered logistic regression, random forests, gradient boosting, and AdaBoost. We primarily optimized feature selection strategies and model fitting parameters. A detailed description of the combinations of models and parameters optimized is available in Table 5 in the Appendix, and selected parameters are detailed in Table 6. The experiments were implemented with Python 3.9.15 and Scikit-learn 1.1.3 [31].

Baseline Models and Evaluation. We evaluated three variants of our model. First of all, we assessed the predictive power of a subset of individual features that have previously been proposed and used for fetal brain QA/QC (namely, `rank_error`, `rank_error_full` `mask_volume`, `centroid`, `centroid_full`, `dl_slice_iqa` and `dl_stack_iqa`). The individual features were scaled and then fitted with a linear regression or logistic regression model for prediction. We then reported the performance of the best-performing feature, which consistently was the `dl_stack_iqa` [27]. Secondly, we considered a BASE variant of our IQA pipeline, using the same subset of features above. Finally, we considered a model using all available features, referred to as FETMRQC.

The models were evaluated on two different data configurations. In the *in-domain* evaluation, we aimed at quantifying how models would generalize on new subjects acquired at either sites. We used nested CV to tune the hyperparameters on the data from one group of subjects from both sites and evaluated the model on a different group of subjects. In the *out-of-domain* evaluation, we aimed at quantifying how models would generalize to new sites. We used nested CV to tune the hyperparameters on the data from one site and evaluated the model on the other site.

Our regression results were evaluated using mean absolute error (MAE) and Spearman rank correlation. Our classification results used F1-score and the area under the receiver operating characteristic curve (AUC ROC).

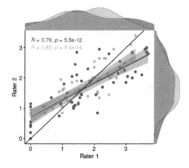
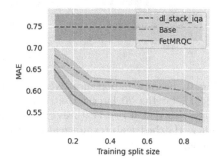

Fig. 4. Inter-rater correlation: blue and yellow data are respectively from CHUV and BCNatal. (Color figure online)

Fig. 5. MAE as a function of the size of the training set. The individual metric, `dl_stack_iqa_full` is constant because it only performs inference.

3   Results and Discussion

FetMRQC's **Reports Optimize Stack Screening and Bolster Inter-rater Reliability.** Figure 4 summarizes the high agreement between the two raters, with a Pearson correlation coefficient of 0.79 and 0.83 for CHUV and BCNatal. On CHUV, 120 series are manually rated below the exclude threshold Quality < 1), and 414 above. On BCNatal, 151 series are rated excluded, and 393 rated above. The total include-to-exclude ratio is 2.98. The total rating time was around 5h 40min for Rater 1 (median of 37 s per volume), and around 6h10 for Rater 2 (median of 40 s per volume).

New IQMs Drive *FetMRQC*'s **Performance.** Tables 1 and 2 shows that the additional features substantially increase the performance of the models, both in the case of regression and classification, and both in- and out-of-domain.

Table 1. In-domain evaluation

	Regression		Classification	
	MAE (↓)	Spearman (↑)	F1 (↑)	AUC (↑)
dl_stack_iqa	0.72 ± 0.05	0.37 ± 0.11	0.85 ± 0.02	0.53 ± 0.02
Base	0.58 ± 0.05	0.60 ± 0.03	0.88 ± 0.02	0.71 ± 0.06
FetMRQC	**0.53 ± 0.09**	**0.71 ± 0.05**	**0.90 ± 0.02**	**0.77 ± 0.07**

Table 2. Out of domain evaluation

	Regression		Classification	
	MAE (↓)	Spearman (↑)	F1 (↑)	AUC (↑)
dl_stack_iqa	0.75 ± 0.03	0.42 ± 0.10	0.83 ± 0.04	0.57 ± 0.07
Base	0.75 ± 0.01	0.38 ± 0.03	0.85 ± 0.02	0.67 ± 0.06
FetMRQC	**0.68 ± 0.06**	**0.50 ± 0.08**	**0.89 ± 0.01**	**0.77 ± 0.05**

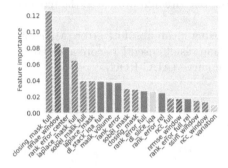
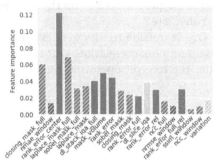

Fig. 6. Feature importance averaged on regression (left) and classification models (right), for the 20 largest contributors. Gray features are not correlated with each other (|corr| < 0.75). Features with the same color are correlated (>0.75) with each other. Hatched features are features that were proposed in this work. (Color figure online)

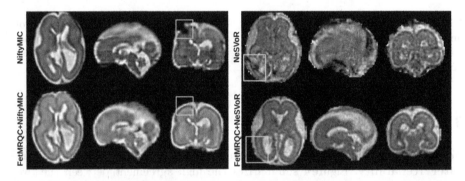

Fig. 7. Illustration of usefulness of QC on the SR reconstruction, using NiftyMIC [18], and NeSVoR [17]. FetMRQC+NiftyMIC successfully removes 6 series out of the 13 available, and FetMRQC+NeSVoR removes 2 out of 5. FetMRQC leads to a substantially greater image quality.

Using More IQMs Allows to Generalize with Fewer Training Data Within Domain. On Fig. 5, we see that not only using more features reduces the overall error on the validation set, but allows to reach a good testing performance using as little as 30% (∼40 subjects, 300 LR series) of the data for training.

***FetMRQC*'s Classifier is Robust When Trained on One Site and Evaluated on the Other.** On Table 2, we see that classification is retained when training on one of the sites and evaluating on the other. Although regression performance is hurt by the domain gap between sizes, our model still generalizes best.

While `dl_stack_iqa` was trained on different data than FetMRQC, the out-of-domain evaluation provides a fair evaluation, where each method is evaluated on a different dataset than the one used for training it (see the acquisition parameters in Table 4).

Different Features Matter for Different Tasks. An advantage of feature-based methods over deep learning-based methods is that their decisions are based on a combination of simple features, which make them more interpretable. On Fig. 6, we see a comparison of the feature importance for regression and classification tasks. These were obtained as by averaging the feature importance for the model selected at each fold of the nested CV. We observe that the importance of features varies largely with the task at hand. While the closing of the brain mask (`closing_mask_full`) and the nMAE are the most predictive of the regression quality), the exclusion of slices relies more on the compressibility of the centermost slices of the image (`rank_error_center`) and the edges of the brain mask (`laplace_mask_full`).

***FetMRQC*'s Classifier Can Drastically Improve the Outcome of SRR Methods.** Figure 7 shows how bad quality stacks can drastically impact the final quality of the SRR, using NiftyMIC [18] and NeSVoR [17]. The images reconstructed without QC displayed significant artifacts. Conversely, the two SRR methods showcased improved quality when subpar stacks were excluded.

4   Conclusion

We propose *FetMRQC*, which adapts the approach of a popular tool, MRIQC, to implement reliable QA/QC of low-resolution stacks of T2w MRI of the fetal brain. Using *FetMRQC* tools, two experts assessed the quality of 1010 stacks with high inter-rater reliability; and these annotations were then applied to automated regression (for QA) and classification (QC). Nested cross-validation of a set of models and hyper-parameters showed how QA and QC can be automated. Objective and reliable QA/QC procedures are critical to ensure the reliability and repeatability of neuroimaging studies, and *FetMRQC* demonstrates how existing approaches can readily be applied on fetal brain MRI.

Appendix

Table 3. Detailed description of the metrics proposed for FetMRQC.

INTENSITY-BASED METRICS	
slice_loss	Use metrics commonly used for outlier rejection [13, 14, 18] to compute the difference between slices in the volume. We consider (normalized) mean averaged error, (normalized) mutual information, normalized cross correlation, (normalized) root mean squared error, peak signal-to-noise ration, structural similarity and joint entropy
sstats [8]	Compute the mean, median, standard deviation, percentiles 5% and 95%, coefficient of variation and kurtosis on brain ROI
entropy [8]	Measure the overall entropy of the image
bias	Level of bias estimated using N4 bias field correction [28]
filter_image	Estimate the sharpness by using Laplace and Sobel filters (commonly used for edge detection)
SHAPED-BASED METRICS	
closing_mask	Morphological closing of the brain mask in the through-plane direction, to detect inter-slice motion. Report the average difference with the original mask
filter_mask	Estimate the sharpness of the brain mask using Laplace and Sobel filtering. In an ideal case, the brain mask would be smoothly varying, especially in the through-plane direction

Table 4. Detailed description of the data from CHUV and BCNatal. Field refers to the magnetic field of the scanner, TR is the repetition time and TE is the echo time and FoV is the Field of View. All scanners used a Half-Fourier Acquisition Single-shot Turbo spin Echo imaging (HASTE) sequence.

	CHUV					
Model (Siemens)	Field [T]	$(n_{\text{subjects}}, n_{\text{LR}})$	TR [ms]	TE [ms]	Resolution [mm³]	FoV [cm]
Aera	1.5	$(34, 281)$	1200	90	$1.12 \times 1.12 \times 3.3$	35.8
MAGNETOM Sola	1.5	$(17, 138)$	1200	90	$1.1 \times 1.1 \times 3.3$	35.8
MAGNETOM Vida	3	$(2, 14)$	1100	101	$0.55 \times 0.55 \times 3$	35.2
Skyra	3	$(8, 77)$	1100	90	$0.55 \times 0.55 \times 3$	35.2
Avanto	1.5	$(1, 5)$	1000	82	$1.2 \times 1.2 \times 4$	30.0
	BCNATAL					
Model (Siemens)	Field [T]	$(n_{\text{subjects}}, n_{\text{LR}})$	TR [ms]	TE [ms]	Resolution [mm³]	FoV [cm]
Aera	1.5	$\mathbf{(16, 158)}$				
		$- (6, 80)$	1500	82	$0.55 \times 0.55 \times 2.5$	28.2
		$- (4, 34)$	1000	137	$0.59 \times 0.59 \times 3.5$	22.7/30.2
		$- (4, 33)$	1000	81	$0.55 \times 0.55 \times 3.15$	28.2
		$- (2, 11)$	1200	94	$1.72 \times 1.72 \times 4.2$	35.8/44.0
MAGNETOM Vida	3	$(11, 56)$	1540	77	$1.04 \times 1.04 \times 3$	20.0
TrioTim	3	$\mathbf{(59, 322)}$				// 4 outliers
		$- (24, 97)$	1100	127	$0.51 \times 0.51 \times 3.5$	26.1
		$- (15, 108)$	990	137	$0.68 \times 0.68 \times 3.5 - 6.0$	26.1
		$- (14, 71)$	2009	137	$0.51 \times 0.51 \times 3.5$	26.1
		$- (1, 14)$	3640	137	$0.51 \times 0.51 \times 3.5$	26.1

Table 5. Parameters automatically optimized by the inner loop of the nested CV.

Model step	Parameters
Remove correlated features	Threshold $\in \{0.8, 0.9\}$; Disabled
Data Scaling	Standard scaling, Robust scaling, No scaling
Winnow algorithm	Enabled, Disabled
PCA	Enabled, Disabled
Regression models	Linear regression, Gradient boosting, Random Forest
Classification models	Logistic regression, Random Forest, Gradient Boosting, AdaBoost

Table 6. Selected hyperparameters for the different nested cross validation procedures. The in-domain experiment uses 5-fold nested cross-validation, while the out-of-domain experiment splits data by site (CHUV and BCNatal) and as a result has only two folds. The list of possible parameters is provided in Table 5.

In-domain – Regression

	Remove feat.	Scaling	Winnow	PCA	Model
BASE	✗	Standard	✓	✓	Random Forest
	0.9	Standard	✓	✗	Random Forest
	0.8	Standard	✓	✗	Random Forest
	0.8	Standard	✓	✗	Gradient Boosting
	0.8	Standard	✓	✗	Random Forest
FETMRQC	✗	Robust	✓	✓	Random Forest
	✗	Robust	✓	✓	Gradient Boosting
	0.8	None	✓	✗	Random Forest
	0.9	Robust	✓	✗	Gradient Boosting
	✗	None	✓	✗	Random Forest

In-domain – Classification

	Remove feat.	Scaling	Winnow	PCA	Model
BASE	0.8	Robust	✓	✓	Random Forest
	✗	None	✓	✓	Random Forest
	✗	Standard	✓	✗	Random Forest
	0.8	Standard	✓	✗	Random Forest
	✗	Standard	✓	✗	Random Forest
FETMRQC	✗	Standard	✓	✓	Gradient Boosting
	0.9	Robust	✓	✓	Random Forest
	0.8	Robust	✓	✗	Gradient Boosting
	0.9	Standard	✓	✓	Lin. Regression
	✗	Standard	✓	✗	Gradient Boosting

Out-of-domain – Regression

	Remove feat.	Scaling	Winnow	PCA	Model
BASE	0.9	Robust	✓	✗	Gradient Boosting
	✗	None	✓	✓	Random Forest
FETMRQC	0.9	None	✓	✓	Lin. Regression
	✗	Robust	✓	✗	Random Forest

Out-of-domain – Classification

	Remove feat.	Scaling	Winnow	PCA	Model
BASE	0.8	Standard	✓	✗	Random Forest
	0.8	Standard	✓	✓	Random Forest
FETMRQC	0.9	Standard	✓	✗	Random Forest
	0.8	Standard	✓	✗	Random Forest

Table 7. Correlation matrix between all 75 IQMs, evaluated on the entire dataset. Blue refers to negative correlations, and red to positive ones.

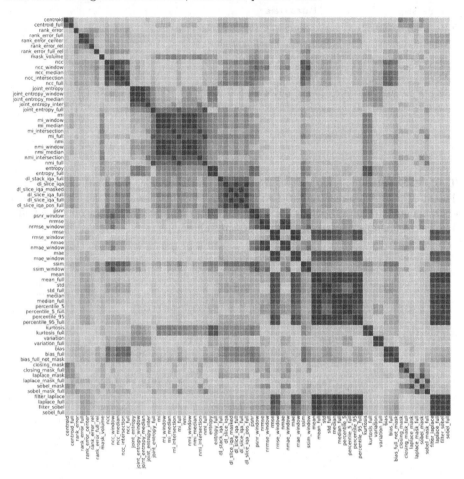

References

1. Gholipour, A., et al.: Fetal MRI: a technical update with educational aspirations. Conc. Magn. Reson. Part A **43**(6), 237–266 (2014)
2. Saleem, S.N.: Fetal MRI: an approach to practice: a review. J. Adv. Res. **5**(5), 507–523 (2014)
3. Power, J.D., et al.: Spurious but systematic correlations in functional connectivity MRI networks arise from subject motion. Neuroimage **59**(3), 2142–2154 (2012)
4. Reuter, M., et al.: Head motion during MRI acquisition reduces gray matter volume and thickness estimates. Neuroimage **107**, 107–115 (2015)
5. Alexander-Bloch, A., et al.: Subtle in-scanner motion biases automated measurement of brain anatomy from in vivo MRI. Hum. Brain Mapp. **37**(7), 2385–2397 (2016)

6. Mortamet, B., et al.: Automatic quality assessment in structural brain magnetic resonance imaging. Magn. Reson. Med. **62**(2), 365–372 (2009)
7. Niso, G., Botvinik-Nezer, R., et al.: Open and reproducible neuroimaging: from study inception to publication. NeuroImage, 119623 (2022)
8. Esteban, O., et al.: MRIQC: advancing the automatic prediction of image quality in MRI from unseen sites. PLoS ONE **12**(9), e0184661 (2017)
9. Klapwijk, E.T., et al.: Qoala-t: a supervised-learning tool for quality control of freesurfer segmented MRI data. Neuroimage **189**, 116–129 (2019)
10. Vogelbacher, C., et al.: Lab-qa2go: a free, easy-to-use toolbox for the quality assessment of magnetic resonance imaging data. Front. Neurosci. **13**, 688 (2019)
11. Samani, Z.R., et al.: Qc-automator: deep learning-based automated quality control for diffusion MR images. Front. Neurosci. **13**, 1456 (2020)
12. Garcia, M., et al.: BrainQCNet: a deep learning attention-based model for multi-scale detection of artifacts in brain structural mri scans. bioRxiv (2022)
13. Kuklisova-Murgasova, M., et al.: Reconstruction of fetal brain MRI with intensity matching and complete outlier removal. Med. Image Anal. **16**(8), 1550–1564 (2012)
14. Kainz, B., et al.: Fast volume reconstruction from motion corrupted stacks of 2D slices. IEEE Trans. Med. Imaging **34**(9), 1901–1913 (2015)
15. Tourbier, S., et al.: Medical-image-analysis-laboratory/mialsuperresolutiontoolkit: MIAL super-resolution toolkit v2.0.1. Zenodo (2020). https://zenodo.org/record/4392788
16. Uus, A., et al.: Retrospective motion correction in foetal MRI for clinical applications: existing methods, applications and integration into clinical practice. Br. J. Radiol. **95**, 20220071 (2022)
17. Xu, J., et al.: NeSVoR: implicit neural representation for slice-to-volume reconstruction in MRI. IEEE Trans. Med. Imaging **42**, 1707–1719 (2023)
18. Ebner, M., et al.: An automated framework for localization, segmentation and super-resolution reconstruction of fetal brain MRI. NeuroImage **206**, 116324 (2020)
19. Uus, A.U., et al.: Automated 3d reconstruction of the fetal thorax in the standard atlas space from motion-corrupted MRI stacks for 21–36 weeks ga range. Med. Image Anal. **80**, 102484 (2022)
20. Lala, S., et al.: A deep learning approach for image quality assessment of fetal brain mri. In: ISMRM, Québec, Canada, Montréal, p. 839 (2019)
21. Xu, J., et al.: Semi-supervised learning for fetal brain MRI quality assessment with ROI consistency. In: Martel, A.L., et al. (eds.) MICCAI 2020. LNCS, vol. 12266, pp. 386–395. Springer, Cham (2020). https://doi.org/10.1007/978-3-030-59725-2_37
22. Liao, L., et al.: Joint image quality assessment and brain extraction of fetal MRI using deep learning. In: Martel, A.L., et al. (eds.) MICCAI 2020. LNCS, vol. 12266, pp. 415–424. Springer, Cham (2020). https://doi.org/10.1007/978-3-030-59725-2_40
23. Gagoski, B., et al.: Automated detection and reacquisition of motion-degraded images in fetal haste imaging at 3 t. Magn. Reson. Med. **87**(4), 1914–1922 (2022)
24. Gorgolewski, K.J., et al.: The brain imaging data structure, a format for organizing and describing outputs of neuroimaging experiments. Sci. Data **3**(1), 1–9 (2016)
25. Ranzini, M., et al.: Monaifbs: monai-based fetal brain MRI deep learning segmentation. arXiv preprint arXiv:2103.13314, 2021
26. de Dumast, P. et al.: Translating fetal brain magnetic resonance image super-resolution into the clinical environment. In: European Congress of Magnetic Resonance in Neuropediatrics (2020)
27. Legoretta, I., Samal, S., et al.: Github repository: automatic fetal brain MRI quality assessment. https://github.com/FNNDSC/pl-fetal-brain-assessment

28. Tustison, N., et al.: N4itk: improved N3 bias correction. IEEE Trans. Med. Imaging **29**(6), 1310–1320 (2010)
29. Littlestone, N.: Learning quickly when irrelevant attributes abound: a new linear-threshold algorithm. Mach. Learn. **2**, 285–318 (1988)
30. Varoquaux, G., et al.: Assessing and tuning brain decoders: cross-validation, caveats, and guidelines. Neuroimage **145**, 166–179 (2017)
31. Pedregosa, F., et al.: Scikit-learn: machine learning in Python. J. Mach. Learn. Res. **12**, 2825–2830 (2011)

A Deep Learning Approach for Segmenting the Subplate and Proliferative Zones in Fetal Brain MRI

Helena S. Sousa[1]([✉]), Abi Fukami-Gartner[2,3]([✉]), Alena U. Uus[1],
Vanessa Kyriakopoulou[2], Brigita Ziukaite[2], Isa Anzak[2],
Jonathan O'Muircheartaigh[2,3], Joseph V. Hajnal[1,2], J-Donald Tournier[1],
Alexander Hammers[1,4], Mary A. Rutherford[2,3], and Maria Deprez[1]

[1] School of Biomedical Engineering and Imaging Sciences, King's College London,
St. Thomas' Hospital, London, UK
helena.sousa@kcl.ac.uk
[2] Centre for the Developing Brain, King's College London, London, UK
abi.gartner@kcl.ac.uk
[3] MRC Centre for Neurodevelopmental Disorders, Institute of Psychiatry,
Psychology and Neuroscience, King's College London, London, UK
[4] King's College London & Guy's and St Thomas' PET Centre, London, UK

Abstract. *In vivo* fetal brain MRI is employed in clinical practice and in research studies to appreciate *in utero* brain development. There is increasing interest in transient regions of the fetal brain, such as the subplate (SP), ventricular zone (VZ) and ganglionic eminence (GE) (also referred to as *germinal matrix*), and their role in normal and abnormal antenatal brain development. On T1w and T2w fetal MRI, these transient regions are defined by highly heterogeneous and stratified signal intensities with rapidly changing patterns. In this work, we define the SP, VZ and GE in a 0.5mm isotropic resolution atlas from the developing Human Connectome Project (dHCP) [1,17,18], and train an Attention U-Net [12] to automatically segment them based on semi-automatically generated labels. Our solution spans from 21 through to 36 weeks gestational age (GA), offering insight into a crucial period of antenatal brain development. The proposed automated segmentation achieved mean Dice scores of 0.88, 0.70 and 0.82 for SP, VZ and GE respectively. A volumetric comparison of transient regions in a small cohort of fetuses with isolated ventriculomegaly (VM, n = 8) vs. controls (n = 265) showed significantly enlarged absolute volumes in the GE (P = 0.005) and VZ (P < 0.001) of the left hemisphere.

Keywords: Fetal brain MRI · Subplate · Ganglionic Eminence · Germinal Matrix · Ventricular Zone · Brain maturation · Automated Segmentation

---

H.S. Sousa and A. Fukami-Gartner—Joint first authors H.S.S an A.F-G contributed equally to this work.

D. Link-Sourani et al. (Eds.): PIPPI 2023, LNCS 14246, pp. 17–27, 2023.
https://doi.org/10.1007/978-3-031-45544-5_2

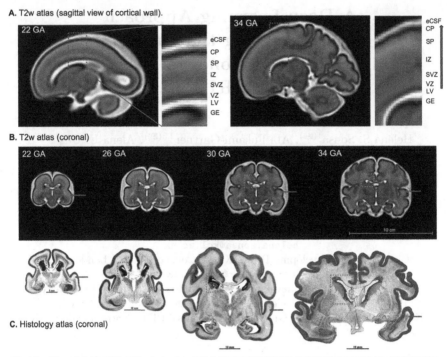

A. T2w atlas (sagittal view of cortical wall).

B. T2w atlas (coronal)

C. Histology atlas (coronal)

Abbreviations: CP = cortical plate; eCSF = extracerebral cerebrospinal fluid; GE = ganglionic eminence; IZ = intermediate zone; LV = lateral ventricles; SP = subplate; SVZ = sub-ventricular zone; VZ = ventricular zone.

Fig. 1. Sagittal (A) and coronal views (B) of T2w fetal brain atlas [1,17]. Red dotted boxes in (A) show stratified intensities in the PZ and WM, which align with known histological layers. (B) and (C) show complimentary coronal views of MRI and histological Nissl stains (adapted from [3,4,8]). Green dotted boxes show parts of the GE and VZ surrounding the LVs. Blue arrows illustrate an example of the SP in the superior temporal gyrus. *GA = weeks gestational age.* (Color figure online)

1   Introduction

In vivo fetal brain MRI can provide complementary diagnostic information to antenatal ultrasound [15], allowing for a detailed characterisation of normal and abnormal patterns of *in utero* brain development based on both qualitative visual analysis and quantitative (e.g., 2D linear and 3D volumetric) biometry. During the second half of pregnancy, T1- and T2-weighted (T1w and T2w) signal intensities of the fetal white matter (WM) and proliferative zones (PZ) are highly heterogeneous and stratified, with rapidly changing patterns. These signal intensities are thought to be related to dynamic cellular processes, such as cell proliferation, differentiation and migration, as well as axonal growth, migration and pre-myelination [10]. Figure 1A showcases the range of stratified WM and PZ intensities at 22 and 34 weeks GA in a T2w fetal brain atlas with an 0.5mm isotropic pixel resolution [1,17,18], which align with known histological layers of the developing cortical wall [10].

Transient Fetal Compartments: The *subplate* (SP) is a transient layer that develops beneath the cortical plate (CP) and above the intermediate zone (IZ) [Fig. 1]. It reaches its peak thickness around mid-gestation (i.e., 20 GA) and gradually resolves at different rates depending on the cortical region. It is composed of numerous neuronal and glial cell types, as well as growing axons, surrounded by an abundance of water-rich extracellular matrix [10]. It has been hypothesised that disturbance to the SP during fetal brain development may be a pathogenic feature in a variety of neurodevelopmental disorders [10]. *Proliferative zones* (PZ) refer to transient compartments of the fetal brain that are principally composed of proliferating neural progenitor cells [10]. In this work, we segmented the *ganglionic eminence* (GE) (also known as the *germinal matrix*) and the ventricular zone (VZ), but excluded the sub-ventricular zone (SVZ) due to its more diffuse signal on MRI. The VZ follows a periventricular distribution, forming a continuous layer of tissue that envelops the lateral ventricles (LV) from all sides, excluding the septum of the cavum septum pellucidum (CSP) and stopping prior to the foramen of Monro [3,4] [Fig. 1]. The GE is a particularly thick and bulbous (i.e., ganglionic) portion of the VZ. It is often subdivided into lateral-, medial- and caudal- areas, which are known to produce distinct sub-types of excitatory and inhibitory neurons [10]. Anomalies within the PZ may result in insufficient cell proliferation and/or migration with important clinical consequences in postnatal life [16]. The GE is also the most common site for neonatal intracerebral haemorrhage (i.e. *germinal matrix haemorrhage*, GMH), particularly following preterm delivery [16].

Related Work: Current publicly available automated deep learning solutions for segmentation of the fetal brain MRI delineate the fetal WM as a single tissue component, often including proliferative regions [13,18]. To the best of our knowledge, only Gholipour et al. [7,11] have successfully sub-segmented the fetal WM and PZ into transient layers from approximately 20 to 30 weeks gestational age (GA) using a fetal brain atlas with 1mm isotropic resolution and classical label propagation.

Contributions: In this work, we propose a deep-learning solution for the automated segmentation of the SP, VZ and GE in fetal T2w MRI from 21 to 36 GA. This expands on the already existing solution for the parcellation of main tissue types in fetal brain MRI (referred to as *BOUNTI*) [18]. We assess the feasibility of using the proposed segmentation for transient regions based on (1) the characterisation of normal spatiotemporal evolution of transient regional volumes (left and right, L/R) in a cohort of 265 healthy fetal subjects (*controls*) and (2) a comparison of 8 subjects with isolated fetal ventriculomegaly (VM) against a robust normative control population.

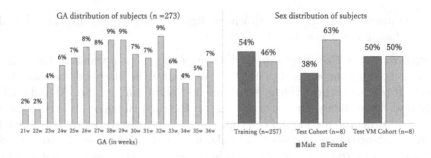

Fig. 2. (A.) GA at scan (in weeks) for all fetal subjects (n = 273) and (B.) sex distribution of (1.) the training dataset (n = 257), (2.) the testing dataset (n = 8) and (3.) fetal subjects with ventriculomegaly (VM, n = 8).

2   Methods

2.1   Cohort, Datasets and Preprocessing

This study used T2w fetal brain MRI acquired as a part of the developing human connectome project (dHCP) public data release [REC 14/LO/1169] [1]. Participants included 265 healthy subjects (*controls*), and 8 subjects with incidental findings of isolated fetal ventriculomegaly (*VM*), scanned between 21-36 GA (Fig. 2). Healthy subjects were divided into 257 subjects for training, and 8 subjects for testing the segmentation network (scanned at 22-, 24-, 26-, 28 -, 30-, 32-, 34-, 36-weeks GA) selected based on GA and good visibility of transient regions on T2w MRI. The age and sex distribution of the cohorts for training and testing the network are shown in Fig. 2. Image acquisition was performed on a 3T Philips Achieva MRI system with a 32-channel cardiac coil, using the dHCP fetal acquisition protocol [14], with TE = 250 ms, resolution of 1.1 × 1.1 mm, slice thickness of 2.2 mm (with −1.1 mm gap), and 6 stacks. The dataset was reconstructed to 0.5mm isotropic pixel resolution using the method of [6] and reoriented to the standard radiological space [21]. Further preprocessing of the datasets for training and testing included brain masking, cropping of the background and resampling the data with padding to a 256 × 256 × 256 grid.

2.2   Neuroanatomical Parcellation of Transient Regions

Semi-automated Generation of Initial Labels for Refinement: The initial segmentation labels for manual refinement of transient regions were obtained as per Fig. 3. The WM label from BOUNTI [18] was used to create new sub-labels for each week from 21–36 GA in atlas space. *For the SP:* WM in the T2w atlas was thresholded by the mean intensity plus one standard deviation (SD) of the WM to keep the highest signal intensities only. *For the GE:* WM in the T1w/T2w ratio atlas was thresholded by the mean intensity plus one SD of the WM to keep the highest signal intensities. This label was further masked to exclude any overlap with the LVs and CSP. *For the VZ:* A mask of the edge of the LVs was created for each week using Scikit-image library (*find boundaries* tool with default parameters) [20] and dilated (parameters set to default) using MIRTK toolbox [2]. The dilated edge label was then masked with the existing LVs and CSP from BOUNTI. Additionally, for SP and GE, smoothing (sigma parameter set to 0.6) and extracting connected components steps (parameters set to default) were applied using MIRTK [2], to remove isolated regions of tissues that did not belong to SP or GE. Any other remaining isolated tissues were manually removed.

Defining Tissue Boundaries on MRI Using Histological Atlases: Nissl stains from the Bayer & Altman [3,4] and Griffiths et al. atlases [8] were compiled for each GA (in the coronal plane, and where available, axial plane) in order to carefully determine the inner and outer boundaries of each transient region on fetal MRI. Figure 1B and 1C illustrate complimentary MRI and Nissl coronal sections at four key timepoints.

Manual Refinement in Atlas Space: Manual refinement was conducted by an experienced researcher with histological knowledge (A.F-Gartner) using ITK-SNAP [22]. Refinement was conducted in atlas space for all weeks from 21–36 GA in an iterative week-by-week process. *For the SP:* Draft SP segmentations were

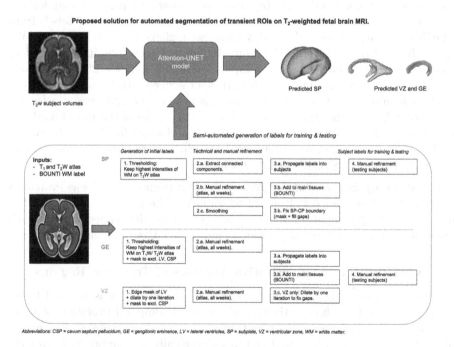

Fig. 3. Proposed solution for the automated segmentation of transient regions of interest (ROIs) on T2w fetal brain MRI based on semi-automated generation of labels for testing & training an Attention U-net [12].

smoothed, masked with the existing cortical GM (cGM) label from BOUNTI and the SP-cGM boundary was filled where needed. *For the GE & VZ:* the GE was refined entirely manually. Draft GE and VZ segmentations were displayed in the same space and any errors at tissue interfaces were corrected. After appropriate technical refinement steps, all transient regions were quality controlled (QC) manually to ensure spatiotemporal accuracy between weeks.

Label Propagation and Manual Refinement in Subject Space: Manually refined labels were propagated from atlas- to subject- space by applying pre-existing subject-specific warps using the FSL package [9] (*applywarp* tool using nearest-neighbour interpolation). Propagated labels for the 8 testing subjects were carefully refined and corrected to create ground truth labels, while labels for the training (n = 257) were not.

2.3   Automated Segmentation of Transient Regions

We propose a 3D segmentation model to jointly segment 25 L/R fetal brain labels, including the proposed transient regions for T2w fetal brain MRI. The segmentation labels for training and testing the network were generated according to the pipeline described in Sect. 2.2 and summarised in Fig. 3.

Network Architecture and Training: Recently, a deep neural network segmentation protocol (BOUNTI [18]) has been shown to perform well for 3D multi-label segmentation of the fetal brain. Here, we extend the 19 labels from BOUNTI to include an additional 3 transient regions (i.e., 6 L/R labels). We share the architecture of BOUNTI (an Attention U-net [12]) implemented in the MONAI framework [5], with an input size of $256 \times 256 \times 256$ and 25 output channels (corresponding to each L/R label segmented). Parameters for the model's architecture, loss functions, optimisers and hyperparameter selection was done following the values described in [18]. Training of the model used 231 images and 26 for validation. The training was performed for 200,000 iterations with the same data augmentations used in [18], plus random crop of training images in patches of size $128 \times 128 \times 128$.

Evaluation of Segmentation Network: The trained model was evaluated on 8 healthy test subjects (from 22 to 36 GA). The performance was tested quantitatively by comparing predicted labels to manually refined ground truth labels using Dice score, recall, precision, and the relative difference in volume.

2.4   Qualitative and Quantitative Analyses of Transient Regions

The feasibility of using the proposed segmentation pipeline was assessed based on (1) a qualitative characterisation of the spatiotemporal evolution of transient regions in atlas space (2) a quantitative characterisation of transient region absolute and relative volumes (L/R) in 265 typically developing fetal subjects from 21 to 36 GA, and (3) a statistical comparison of absolute and relative transient volumes for 8 subjects with VM against controls (n = 265) using the *extra-sum-of-squares F test.*

3 Results and Discussion

3.1 Qualitative Analysis of Transient Regions in Atlas Space

Figure 4 shows 3D renderings of the SP, GE and VZ segmentations from 22 to 34 weeks GA in atlas space. The existing publicly available automated segmentation solution for transient regions stops at 30 GA [7], missing a crucial period of late antenatal brain development. From a qualitative and morphological perspective, the SP (in blue) forms a thick and continuous layer under the CP around mid-gestation (e.g., 22 GA), but gradually resolves in sulcal pits as cortical gyrification rapidly progresses from 30 to 36 GA. The thin layer of VZ tissue (in yellow) lining the LVs continues to grow at the same pace as the LVs, and we do not notice any major shape change, other than areas of gradual thinning particularly from 34 GA. Finally, the GE (in green) also grows in absolute size, as the whole brain size grows antenatally. However, there is a visible thinning of the caudal GE (CGE) prior to the medial- (MGE) and lateral- (LGE) portions.

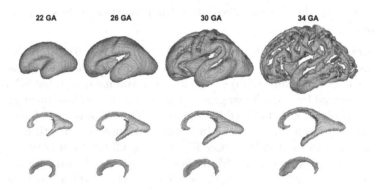

Fig. 4. 3D rendering of SP (in blue), VZ (in yellow) and GE (in green) in atlas space at 22-, 26-, 30- and 34-weeks GA. (Color figure online)

3.2 Quantitative Analyses of Transient Regions in Subject Space

Quantitative Evaluation of Network Performance: Fig. 5 shows the quantitative evaluation of network performance. The network detected all transient regions in all test subjects and showed consistency in results for L/R sides in all metrics. This was confirmed by relatively high Dice scores for all regions (0.87 and 0.88 for L/R SP, 0.82 and 0.81 for L/R GE and 0.70 for both L/R VZ), which are in agreement with the recall and precision scores. We note that, as expected, the VZ (L/R) show the lowest DICE scores due to their very thin

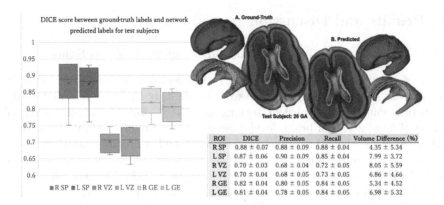

Fig. 5. Quantitative evaluation of network predicted labels against ground truth labels for 8 testing subjects. The metrics (Dice, recall, precision and volume difference) were calculated for L/R transient region labels. Example labels over T2w image and 3D renderings for (A.) ground truth and (B.) predicted labels for a test subject at 26GA.

nature enveloping the LVs (approximately 1mm thickness or less, depending on the region).

Volumetric Development of Transient Regions in Healthy Controls:
Fig. 6 illustrates the normal volumetric development of transient regions (L/R) from 21 to 36 GA in healthy subjects. In absolute volume (cm^3), the SP and VZ were characterised by a non-linear growth curve, and showed fast growth from 21 to approximately 34 GA, followed by a plateau. The GE was best characterised by a linear regression showing slow incremental volumetric growth from 21 to 36 GA. Relative to total WM volume (% of WM), all transient regions showed a decline in relative volume. The SP decline was best fitted with a linear regression, whilst the VZ and GE showed a non-linear decline, which was faster from approximately 21 to 30 GA. The predicted volumes for the 8 testing subjects did not show any major deviation from the total training cohort (group difference, *ns*), validating the performance of network prediction on unseen data.

3.3   Quantitative Comparison of Transient Volumes in Fetuses with Ventriculomegaly and Controls

Absolute and relative transient regional volumes (L/R) were fitted with the most appropriate regression model (i.e. linear or non-linear) in order to compute the *extra-sum-of-squares F test* [Fig. 7]. Left VZ volumes were significantly enlarged in the VM cohort in absolute (P < 0.001) and relative (P = 0.0026) terms. The left GE was also significantly larger in absolute (P = 0.0051) and relative (P = 0.028) volume. The SP did not show any significant differences between the VM and control cohorts (*data not shown*). For the VZ and GE, we calculated the % difference of L vs R regions for each VM and testing subject and conducted an unpaired t-test for group difference. For VM subjects, the left VZ was on

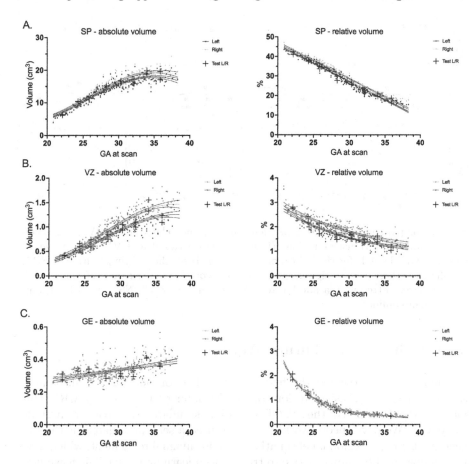

Fig. 6. Normal temporal evolution of transient volumes (L/R) from 21 to 36 GA. Absolute (in cm^3, left column) and relative (% of WM, right column) volumes extracted from network prediction for 257 training (*coloured dots*) and 8 testing subjects (*crosses*) fitted with a non-linear regression and 95 % CI. Row (A.) SP, (B.) VZ and (C.) GE.

average 19.5% larger than the right, which was significantly different compared to testing subjects (P = 0.006). Similarly, the left GE was on average 7.9% larger than the right, which was also significantly different between groups (P = 0.04). These results were confirmed by visually inspecting predicted labels in the VM cohort, which was composed of 6 cases with left unilateral VM (75%) (which is clinically more frequent) and 2 cases with bilateral VM (25%). Our results were in line with the existing fetal VM literature[19].

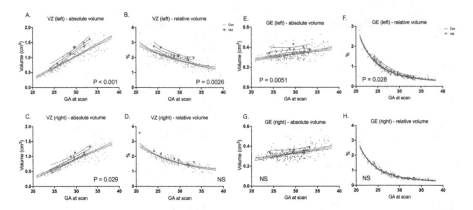

Fig. 7. Comparison of absolute (cm^3, left column) and relative (% of WM, right column) volumes for transient regions (L/R) in control (*dots*) and VM (*red triangles*) subjects. Graphs A-D for the VZ (in orange) and E-H for the GE (in green). The SP is not shown as there were no significant differences. Volumes were extracted from network prediction and fitted with a non-linear regression and 95 % CI. NS = non-significant. (Color figure online)

4   Conclusion and Future Work

In summary, we presented the first deep-learning solution for the automated segmentation of 3 transient regions of the developing fetal brain on MRI. This included the definition of the SP, GE and VZ in standard atlas space from 21–36 weeks GA. We developed a workflow, which used a semi-automated method to generate transient region labels in atlas space for manual refinement, which were then propagated to subject space to train a deep-learning model. The feasibility of using a deep-learning network to segment transient regions was confirmed via (1) a characterisation of normal volumetric development from 21–36 GA and (2) a volumetric analysis of transient regions in fetuses with VM, which highlighted significantly enlarged left VZ and GE volumes. Future work will involve conducting an inter-rater analysis to guarantee the consistency of manually refined transient region labels between researchers, thereby also enhancing the reliability of the automatic segmentation network. Moreover, to further enhance the performance of the network, we suggest incorporating diverse cohorts (featuring distinct image acquisition protocols and clinical conditions) into the network's training. This approach aims to fortify the network's robustness, reduce bias, and potentially demonstrate its clinical relevance as an early diagnostic automated image analysis tool.

Acknowledgments. We would like to thank all participating mothers & families and staff involved in the dHCP. AF-G.'s PhD research is funded by the MRC CNDD, and H.S.S by the EPSRC CDT in Smart Medical Imaging (EP/S022104/1). This research project was supported by the Academy of Medical Sciences Springboard Award (SBF0041040), ERC under the European Union's Seventh Framework Programme [FP7/ 20072013]/ERC grant 319456 (dHCP), Wellcome/EPSRC Centre for Medical Engineering at KCL [WT 203148/Z/16/Z)], the NIHR CRF at Guy's and St Thomas'. The views expressed are those of the authors and not necessarily those of the NHS, the NIHR, or the Department of Health and Social Care.

References

1. Developing human connectome project. http://www.developingconnectome.org
2. Mirtk software package. https://github.com/BioMedIA/MIRTK
3. Bayer, S.A., Altman, J.: The Human Brain During the Third Trimester. CRC Press (2003)
4. Bayer, S.A., Altman, J.: The human brain during the second trimester (2005)
5. Cardoso, M.J., et al.: Monai: An open-source framework for deep learning in healthcare. arXiv preprint arXiv:2211.02701 (2022)
6. Cordero-Grande, L., et al.: Automating motion compensation in 3T fetal brain imaging: localize, align and reconstruct. In: ISMRM 2019, p. 1000 (2019)
7. Gholipour, A., et al.: A normative spatiotemporal MRI atlas of the fetal brain for automatic segmentation and analysis of early brain growth. Sci. Rep. 7 (2017)
8. Griffiths, P.D., et al.: Sectional anatomy of the fetal brain (2010)
9. Jenkinson, M., et al.: FSl. Neuro Image **62**(2), 782–790 (2012)
10. Kostović, I., et al.: Neural histology and neurogenesis of the human fetal and infant brain. Neuro Image **188**, 743–773 (2019)
11. Machado-Rivas, F., et al.: Normal growth, sexual dimorphism, and lateral asymmetries at fetal brain MRI. Radiology **303**, 162–170 (2022)
12. Oktay, O., et al.: Attention U-Net: learning where to look for the pancreas. In: MIDDL 2016 (2018)
13. Payette, K., et al.: An automatic multi-tissue human fetal brain segmentation benchmark using the fetal tissue annotation dataset. Sci. Data **8** (2021)
14. Price, A.N., et al.: The developing human connectome project (DHCP): fetal acquisition protocol. In: ISMRM 2019 (2019)
15. Rutherford, M., et al.: MR imaging methods for assessing fetal brain development (2008)
16. Stuempflen, M., et al.: The ganglionic eminence: volumetric assessment of transient brain structure utilizing fetal magnetic resonance imaging. Ultrasound in Obstet. & Gynecol. (2023)
17. Uus, A., et al.: Multi-channel spatio-temporal MRI atlas of the normal fetal brain development from the developing human connectome project. G-Node (2023)
18. Uus, A.U., et al.: Bounti: brain volumetry and automated parcellation for 3D fetal MRI. biorxiv (2023)
19. Vasung, L., et al.: Abnormal development of transient fetal zones in mild isolated fetal ventriculomegaly. Cereb. Cortex (2022)
20. Van der Walt, S., et al.: scikit-image: image processing in Python. PeerJ **2**, e453 (2014)
21. Wright, R., et al.: LSTM spatial co-transformer networks for registration of 3D Fetal US and MR brain images. In: PIPPI/DATRA -2018. LNCS, vol. 11076, pp. 149–159. Springer, Cham (2018). https://doi.org/10.1007/978-3-030-00807-9_15
22. Yushkevich, P.A., et al.: User-guided 3D active contour segmentation of anatomical structures: significantly improved efficiency and reliability. Neuro Image **31**, 1116–1128 (2006)

Combined Quantitative T2* Map and Structural T2-Weighted Tissue-Specific Analysis for Fetal Brain MRI: Pilot Automated Pipeline

Alena U. Uus[1(✉)], Megan Hall[2], Kelly Payette[2], Joseph V. Hajnal[1,2], Maria Deprez[1], Mary A. Rutherford[2], Jana Hutter[1,2], and Lisa Story[2,3]

[1] Biomedical Engineering Department, King's College London, St. Thomas' Hospital, London SE1 7EH, UK
`alena.uus@kcl.ac.uk`
[2] Centre for the Developing Brain, King's College London, London, UK
[3] Academic Women's Health Department, King's College London, London, UK

Abstract. Over the past decade, automated 3D reconstruction and segmentation has been widely applied to processing and analysis of fetal MRI. While the majority of reported methods primarily focus on structural brain imaging, additional quantitative T2* information could improve characterisation of changes in functional tissue properties. In this work, we propose a first solution for automated combined tissue-specific analysis of 3D quantitative T2* map and structural T2-weighted (T2w) fetal brain MRI. We build upon the existing 3D structural brain analysis pipeline from SVRTK by adding fully automated 3D T2* reconstructions globally aligned to 3D segmented T2w images (already reconstructed in the standard radiological space) followed by deep learning T2* tissue parcellation. In addition, we assess the general applicability the proposed pipeline by analysing brain growth trajectories in 26 control T2w+T2* fetal MRI datasets from 20–28 weeks GA range.

Keywords: Fetal MRI · Multi-contrast alignment · Automated segmentation · Brain T2* · Tissue parcellation

1 Introduction

Fetal MRI allows detailed characterisation of normal and abnormal patterns of fetal brain development [12,14]. Recent advances in retrospective motion correction techniques [19] based on automated 3D slice-to-volume registration (SVR) reconstruction for structural T2w MRI allow true 3D volumetric analysis [15] of fetal brain MRI datasets. In addition to anatomical T2w-based analysis, quantitative T2* fetal MRI provides complementary information that can further improve understanding of functional tissue properties of the developing brain [3,6,21].

© The Author(s), under exclusive license to Springer Nature Switzerland AG 2023
D. Link-Sourani et al. (Eds.): PIPPI 2023, LNCS 14246, pp. 28–38, 2023.
https://doi.org/10.1007/978-3-031-45544-5_3

Automation of structural T2w brain 3D SVR reconstruction has been already addressed in a large number of works with many available alternative deep learning pipelines [5,13,22] with automated masking and reorientation. Furthermore, during the past couple of years there have been multiple reported deep learning solutions for fetal brain parcellation [8,11,20]. However, none of these methods has yet been applied to quantitative fetal brain T2* analysis and the next logical step would be to expand the current pipelines for combined multi-modal MRI assessment of the fetal brain.

Contributions

In this work, we propose a first pilot solution for automated combined tissue-specific analysis of 3D quantitative T2* and structural T2w fetal brain MRI. We build upon the existing 3D T2w structural brain reconstruction and analysis BOUNTI pipeline from the auto SVRTK docker[1] by adding fully automated 3D T2* reconstructions aligned to 3D segmented T2w SVR images in standard radiological space followed by deep learning T2* tissue parcellation. In addition, we explore the practical application of combining volumetric and quantitative information by analysing brain growth trajectories in 26 normal control fetal MRI datasets from the late 2nd trimester.

2   Methods

2.1   Datasets, Acquisition and Pre-processing

This study employed fetal MRI data acquired at St. Thomas' Hospital, London under the "Individualised Risk prediction of adverse neonatal outcome in pregnancies that deliver preterm using advanced MRI techniques and machine learning" study (REC 21/SS/0082), (REC), "Placenta Imaging Project" (REC: 16/LO/1573), "Antenatal assessment of fetal infection utilising advanced MRI protocols" (REC: 19/LO/0736) including 76 datasets of subjects from 20 to 35 weeks GA range without structural brain anomalies from control and preterm birth risk cohorts. All datasets were acquired on 3T Philips Achieva MRI system using a 32-channel cardiac coil. The structural T2w (single-short turbo spin echo sequence) datasets include 5–6 stacks with TE = 180 ms, in-plane resolution 1.25×1.25 mm, slice thickness 2.5 mm and 0/−1.5 mm gap. The relaxometry T2* datasets (gradient echo single-shot echo planar sequence) include 1 stack with five echoes TE = [13–240] ms, TR = 3 s, $1.85 \times 1.85 \times 2$mm resolution. The inclusion criteria were: 20–31 weeks GA range; full brain coverage in the T2w and T2* raw stacks; no significant in-plane slice corruption; no distortion of the brain ROI; no severe signal intensity artifacts; clear appearance of the brain features in T2* map. An in-house Python script was used to generate T2* maps for all input raw stacks using mono-exponential decay fitting [7]. For all datasets, we

---

[1] SVRTK automated fetal MRI reconstruction and segmentation docker: https://hub. docker.com/r/fetalsvrtk/svrtk *auto-2.20* tag.

used the SVRTK docker [1] to process T2w stacks that produced 3D SVR images with 0.85 mm isotropic resolution (automated version of [9]) and BOUNTI brain tissue segmentations [20].

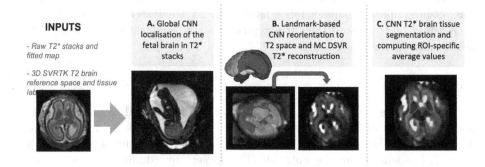

Fig. 1. The proposed automated pipeline for combined 3D T2* SVR reconstruction and segmentation of the fetal brain in the standard 3D structural T2w space.

2.2 Automated 3D T2* Fetal Brain Reconstruction in T2w Space

The proposed pipeline for automated combined T2w+T2* reconstruction of the fetal brain is illustrated in Fig. 1.B. The inputs include raw multi-echo T2* stacks with fitted map and a 3D T2w brain image reconstructed in the standard space using the auto SVRTK docker with BOUNTI brain tissue segmentation [1]. At first, the fetal brain is globally localised in the T2* stacks. Next, the detected T2* brain ROI is reoriented to the standard 3D T2w space using landmark registration approach (the global brain ROI landmarks are automatically segmented in both T2w and T2*). This is followed by additional registration and multi-channel deformable SVR (DSVR) reconstruction of the 2nd echo and T2* map in the T2w space. At the final step, the reconstructed 3D T2* brain map is automatically segmented into the 6 major tissue ROIs for quantitative analysis (in addition to 3D T2w volumetry).

3D Brain Localisation and Masking in T2* Stacks. Similarly to [18], localisation of the fetal brain in raw T2* stacks is based on 3D multi-label CNN segmentation (Fig. 1.A) that already showed robust performance for T2w datasets. We employ the 2nd echo of T2* stacks for segmentation because of the optimal visibility of the fetus and the classical 3D Attention-UNet [10] architecture with 3 output channels (brain, trunk and background) (see Sect. 2.5). We initialised the network with the weights pretrained on T2w datasets from the auto SVRTK docker and trained it on 50 T2* stacks from different GA ranges with manually created 3D labels of the brain and trunk.

3D Reorientation of T2* Fetal Brain ROI to the Standard T2w Space.
After localisation, the brain ROI in the 2nd echo is cropped and passed to the
landmark detection network that segment 5 global brain regions (frontal, back,
central, brainstem+cerebellum, whole brain) (Fig. 1.B). These landmarks were
selected as optimal for point-based registration because of the clear differentiation and visibility at various GA ranges. We used the classical 3D Attention-UNet
network (see Sect. 2.5) initialised with the weights pretrained on T2w datasets
from the auto SVRTK docker. The network was then trained on 50 2nd echo
T2* cropped brain stacks with labels propagated from the aligned 3D T2w brain
datasets.

After segmentation of the brain landmarks they are aligned to the segmented
landmarks in the corresponding 3D T2w SVR reconstructed image using the classical point-based registration [2]. The output transformation is used for initialisation of the additional classical rigid registration (based on normalised mutual
information similarity metric) for further refinement of the T2w/T2* alignment.

**3D Reconstruction of T2* Fetal Brain ROI in the Standard T2w
Space.** Next, the reoriented the 2nd echo and T2* map stacks are used for
reconstruction of the T2* brain ROI using the optimised multi-channel DSVR
function from SVRTK [16,17] with the existing 3D T2w brain image as the template. Taking into account that only one T2* stack is available per dataset we
used only global nonlinear registration, super-resolution replaced with averaging,
no robust statistics and no intensity matching. The reconstruction is followed
by additional FFD-based registration step (local normalised cross-correlation,
7 mm kernel, 10mm control point spacing) of 2nd echo T2* to the masked T2w
image with removed extra-cerebral CSF to improve alignment of the cortex ROI.
The 3D reconstructed output includes 2nd echo and T2* map channels and is
transformed to the standard radiological space of the 3D SVR T2w image with
0.85 mm resolution.

2.3   Automated 3D T2* Fetal Brain Tissue Segmentation

Taking into account the lower resolution and varying regional quality of T2*
datasets as well as the uncertainty of the T2w/T2* alignment, even the perfect
quality brain tissue segmentations of the 3D T2w image cannot be directly used
for analysis of T2* maps. Therefore, we adapted the earlier proposed T2w fetal
brain BOUNTI segmentation protocol [20] based on relevance for quantitative
analysis of solid tissue structures. We combined left and right parcellations into
single compartments and removed extra-cerebral CSF. The resulting protocol
has 6 ROIs: cortical GM, WM, deep GM, ventricles, brainstem and cerebellum.

The segmentation of 3D T2* images is performed using the classical 3D
Attention-UNet architecture (implementation details are given in Sect. 2.5). We
trained the network based on the 3D map channel since it provides the optimal
contrast for brain tissue differentiation for computation of average T2* values.

The ground truth labels were created by using the fused BOUNTI parcellations from aligned T2w+T2* reconstructed brains followed by manual refinement

(guided by both 2nd echo and T2* map channels), when required. At first, the model was pretrained using the T2w contrast. In total, we used 41 training, 4 validation and 8 testing T2* datasets from 20–31 weeks GA range.

The mean T2* values within segmented ROIs were computed as average from the reconstructed 3D maps with additional exclusion of outlier voxels (<2 standard deviations, $< 40\,\text{ms}$ and $> 600\,\text{ms}$).

2.4 Analysis of Brain Development in Combined T2w+T2* Datasets

We selected 26 datasets of normal control subjects from the late 2nd trimester (20–28 weeks GA range) for general assessment of applicability of the proposed approach for quantitative fetal brain MRI studies. All datasets were automatically reconstructed and segmented using the combined T2w (existing SVRTK + BOUNTI) and proposed T2* pipelines. The final segmentation labels were inspected and manually refined, when required. The output tissue-specific T2w volumetry and T2* values were analysed in terms of correlation with GA.

2.5 Implementation Details

All segmentation networks are based on the standard MONAI [4] 3D Attention-UNet [10] implementations with five and four encoder-decoder blocks (output channels 32, 64, 128, 256 and 512), correspondingly, convolution and upsampling kernel size of 3, ReLU activation, dropout ratio of 0.5. We employed AdamW optimiser with a linearly decaying learning rate, initialised at 1×10^{-3}, default β parameters and weight decay $= 1 \times 10^{-5}$. We used the standard MONAI bias field and affine rotations for augmentation. The general preprocessing steps included: cropping of the background, resampling with padding to $128 \times 128 \times 128$ input grid size and rescaling to 0–1.

All preprocessing and reconstruction steps were implemented based on MIRTK[2] toolbox and SVRTK[3] package. The pipeline will be publicly available online as a CPU-based docker at SVRTK docker repository[4] (tag: *auto-brain-t2-t2s*).

3 Experiments and Results

3.1 Automated 3D T2* Fetal Brain Reconstruction in T2w Space

The testing was performed on 8 selected T2+T2* fetal MRI datasets from 21–30 weeks GA in terms of accuracy of brain localisation, masking and reorientation of the fetal brain T2* ROI to the standard 3D T2w space.

---

[2] MIRTK library: https://github.com/BioMedIA/MIRTK.

[3] SVRTK toolbox: https://github.com/SVRTK/SVRTK.

[4] SVRTK docker: https://hub.docker.com/r/fetalsvrtk/svrtk.

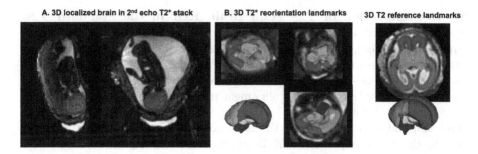

Fig. 2. Visual example of localisation (A) and reorientation labels (B) for 21 weeks GA test dataset (2nd echo T2* stack).

3D Brain Localisation and Masking in T2* Stacks. The results of testing of localisation performance are given in Table 1 in terms of Dice, localisation score (0.0 - fail; 0.5 - partial; 1.0 - correct) and centre-point distance (mm) vs. the ground truth manual labels. The brain was localised successfully in all test T2* stacks. Notably, the network successfully segmented the brain at different GA ranges (Fig. 2.A).

Table 1. Evaluation of CNN-based 3D localisation of the fetal brain in T2* stacks: Dice, localisation QC score and centre-point distance.

Dice	Localisation QC	Centre-point distance (mm)
0.885 ± 0.038	1.00 ± 0.00	3.221 ± 2.116

3D Reorientation of T2* Fetal Brain ROI to the Standard T2w Space. The results of testing of reorientation performance are given in Table 2 in terms of Dice, reorientation QC score (0.0 - fail; 0.5 - partial; 1.0 - correct) and rotation different (degrees) vs. the ground truth manual labels and transformation difference to the 3D T2w space. The brain was successfully reoriented to the standard T2w space in all datasets with <10°C global error. Notably, the network performed well at different GA ranges (Fig. 2.B).

Table 2. Evaluation of CNN 3D landmark-based reorientation of the fetal brain in T2* stacks to 3D T2w space: average Dice (5 reorientation labels), reorientation QC score and transformation rotation difference before and after additional rigid registration.

Average Dice	Reorientation QC	Rotation difference (degree)
0.783 ± 0.061	0.938 ± 0.177	8.257 ± 3.911

3D Reconstruction of T2* Fetal Brain ROI in the Standard T2w Space. The direct assessment of the quality of aligned 3D T2* to T2w reconstruction is challenging due to the intrinsic difference in contrast as well as the spatial distortions present in the original T2* stacks. Qualitative visual inspection confirmed that all test T2* brain images were reconstructed in the standard space with relatively good global alignment to T2w. However, nonlinear spatial distortions could not be resolved by the classical registration. E.g., Fig. 4 shows three longitudinal datasets from the main cohort and the distortion is clearly seen in the 1st example. An additional quantitative comparison between 3D 2nd echo T2* and T2w reconstructions showed acceptable NCC (0.378 ± 0.087) values (for different contrasts).

3.2   Automated 3D T2* Fetal Brain Tissue Segmentation

The results of testing of the T2* brain tissue segmentation network (based on the map channel) for the same 8 subjects are summarised in Fig. 3. The Dice values are within acceptable range for both large and high contrast structures (WM, cerebellum) and average for the cortex ROI GM due to the low contrast. Late GA test cases have lower Dice for the cortex ROI and generally expected to be prone to errors due to the limited visibility of the cortex. The differences of the mean ROI-specific T2* values do not exceed 5% thus potentially confirming the feasibility of using deep learning as initialisation for regional T2* analysis. However, this might be also caused by the suboptimal quality of the manually edited ground truth segmentations used for training and testing. I.e., the cortical segmentation in T2* channel is significantly thicker due to partial volume effect (Fig. 4).

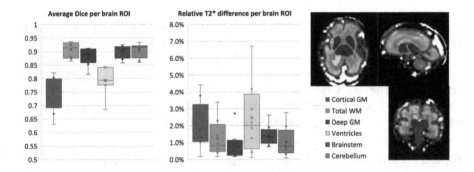

Fig. 3. Quantitative evaluation of T2* brain tissue parcellation network on 8 subjects: Dice and relative T2* difference in segmented brain ROIs.

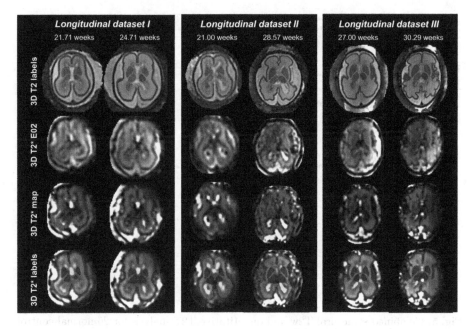

Fig. 4. Visual examples of 3D reconstructed and segmented combined structural T2w and quantitative T2* longitudinal datasets.

3.3 Analysis of Brain Development in T2w+T2* Datasets

The graphs in Fig. 5 show the T2w volumetry and mean T2* for the selected 26 normal cases (20–28 weeks GA). All segmentations were reviewed manually refined in 16 cases (primarily in the cortex and ventricle ROIs). Neither refinement or the choice of voxel outlier limits did not produce significant differences in the trends.

There is the expected increase in T2w-derived volumes for all solid tissue ROIs (cortical GM, WM, deep GM, cerebellum). This is correlated with the decreasing mean T2* values in cortical GM and cerebellum. The T2* values in the WM and deep GM ROIs do not show pronounced trends during this GA range which is consistent with the results reported for the 2nd trimester in the existing 1.5T fetal brain T2* studies [3,6,21].

Notably, there is a pronounced heterogeneity of T2* within the WM ROI Fig. 4 with low values in ganglionic eminence and high values in subplate layers as well as global regional variations (e.g., higher values in frontal lobe). This highlights that an additional parcellation of the WM ROI into transient compartments is required for more detailed tissue-specific quantitative analysis. Furthermore, the average T2* values are also affected by the partial volume effect and both image-space and fitting artifacts that requires an extra step for automated exclusion of these regions.

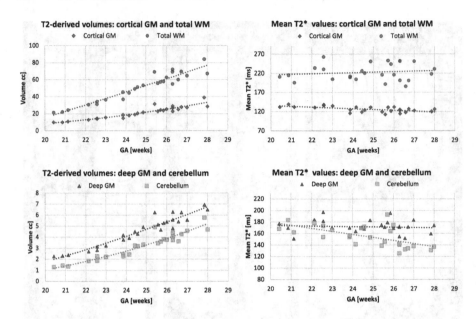

Fig. 5. Combined structural T2w and quantitative T2* analysis for 26 normal control datasets for 20–28 weeks GA range: cortical GM, total WM, deep GM and cerebellum.

4   Discussion and Conclusions

In this work, we presented the pilot automated pipeline for 3D T2w+T2* combined analysis of the fetal brain development. We extended the existing 3D structural brain analysis pipeline from the automated SVRTK docker [1] with automated 3D reconstruction of quantitative T2* aligned to T2w reference space and segmentation of the main solid brain tissue ROIs. The T2* segmentations are used to compute tissue-specific T2* values while the structural T2w parcellation provide volumetric information. This is the first proposed solution for fully automated multi-regional T2* brain segmentation, which is conventionally performed manually [3,6,21].

The proposed deep learning steps for 3D localisation and landmark-based reorientation to the reference T2w space showed robust performance on the test datasets. Yet, the quality of T2w/T2* alignment is not perfect and cannot assessed by definition due to the inherent difference in contrast and resolution and presence of distortion and intensity artifact. In terms of the future work, implementation of deep learning contrast transfer and registration between T2w and T2* should improve both quality and certainty of alignment. Furthermore, in this pilot work, we used only high quality T2* datasets < 31 weeks, while a more robust solution will be required for suboptimal quality cases with low contrast, intensity artifacts, motion and spatial distortions. The proposed pipeline might also contribute to design of acquisition protocols to optimally explore joint T2* and T2w analysis.

The proposed 3D T2* brain tissue parcellation network also provides sufficient results for computation of tissue-specific T2* values with only minimal required manual editing. This is the first step towards minimisation of time-consuming manual segmentation of T2* data. Analysis of 26 normal control datasets indicated potential correlation of changes between the brain tissue T2* and volumetry in cortical GM and cerebellum. However, the investigated GA window was too narrow to capture the full scale of age-related changes in WM T2* (e.g., [6]) and is inconclusive. Further parcellation of the WM ROI into compartments such as subplate, germinal matrix and periventricular zone would also be a significant contribution to the accuracy of quantitative analysis since they have very heterogeneous T2* values. Using multi-channel segmentation that includes the T2* map and T2w channels should also improve segmentation certainty. Our future work will also focus on optimisation for the wider GA range, automated detection and exclusion of outlier voxels and inclusion of anomalies. Additional extensive inter-rater/intra-rater analysis will also be required for assessment of segmentation quality on quantitative data.

Acknowledgments. We thank everyone who was involved in acquisition and analysis of the datasets and all participating mothers and families.

This work was supported by NIHR Advanced Fellowship awarded to Lisa Story [NIHR30166], MRC Confidence in concept [MC_PC_19041], the NIH Human Placenta Project grant [1U01HD087202-01], the Wellcome/ EPSRC Centre for Medical Engineering at King's College London [WT 203148/Z/16/Z], the NIHR Clinical Research Facility (CRF) at Guy's and St Thomas' and by the National Institute for Health Research Biomedical Research Centre based at Guy's and St Thomas' NHS Foundation Trust and King's College London.

The views expressed are those of the authors and not necessarily those of the NHS, the NIHR or the Department of Health.

References

1. Svrtk fetal MRI docker (2023). https://hub.docker.com/r/fetalsvrtk/svrtk
2. Arun, K.S., et al.: Least-squares fitting of two 3-d point sets. IEEE Trans. Pattern Anal. Mach. Intell. PAMI **9**(5), 698–700 (1987)
3. Baadsgaard, K., et al.: T2* weighted fetal MRI and the correlation with placental dysfunction. Placenta **131**, 90–97 (2023)
4. Cardoso, M.J., et al.: Monai: an open-source framework for deep learning in healthcare. arXiv preprint arXiv:2211.02701 (2022)
5. Ebner, M., et al.: An automated framework for localization, segmentation and super-resolution reconstruction of fetal brain MRI. NeuroImage **206**, 116324 (2020)
6. Hall, M., et al.: Characterisation of placental, fetal brain and maternal cardiac structure and function in pre-eclampsia using MRI. medRxiv (2023)
7. Hutter, J., et al.: Multi-modal functional MRI to explore placental function over gestation. Magn. Reson. Med. **81**, 1191–1204 (2019)
8. Karimi, D., et al.: Learning to segment fetal brain tissue from noisy annotations. Med. Image Anal., 102731 (2023)

 9. Kuklisova-Murgasova, M., et al.: Reconstruction of fetal brain MRI with intensity matching and complete outlier removal. MediAN **16**(8), 1550–1564 (2012)
10. Oktay, O., et al.: Attention u-net: learning where to look for the pancreas. In: MIDDL 2016 (2018)
11. Payette, K., et al.: An automatic multi-tissue human fetal brain segmentation benchmark using the fetal tissue annotation dataset. Sci. Data **8**, 1–14 (2021)
12. Prayer, D., et al.: Isuog practice guidelines (updated): performance of fetal magnetic resonance imaging. Ultrasound Obstet. Gynecol. **61**, 278–287 (2023)
13. Salehi, S.S., Khan, S., Erdogmus, D., Gholipour, A.: Real-time deep pose estimation with geodesic loss for image-to-template rigid registration. IEEE TMI **38**(2), 470–481 (2019)
14. Story, L., Rutherford, M.: Advances and applications in fetal magnetic resonance imaging. Obstet. Gynaecol. **17**, 189–199 (2015)
15. Story, L., et al.: Brain volumetry in fetuses that deliver very preterm: an MRI pilot study. NeuroImage: Clin. **30**, 102650 (2021)
16. Uus, A., et al.: Deformable slice-to-volume registration for motion correction of fetal body and placenta MRI. IEEE TMI **39**, 2750–2759 (2020)
17. Uus, A., et al.: Deformable slice-to-volume registration for reconstruction of quantitative t2* placental and fetal MRI, pp. 222–232 (2020)
18. Uus, A.U., et al.: Automated 3d reconstruction of the fetal thorax in the standard atlas space from motion-corrupted MRI stacks for 21–36 weeks GA range. MedIAn **80** (2022)
19. Uus, A.U., et al.: Retrospective motion correction in foetal MRI for clinical applications: existing methods, applications and integration into clinical practice. Brit. J. Radiol. **96**, 20220071 (2022)
20. Uus, A.U., et al.: Bounti: brain volumetry and automated parcellation for 3D fetal MRI. bioRxiv (2023)
21. Vasylechko, S., et al.: T2 relaxometry of fetal brain at 1.5 tesla using a motion tolerant method. Magn. Reson. Med. **73**, 1795–1802 (2015)
22. Xu, J., et al.: Nesvor: implicit neural representation for slice-to-volume reconstruction in MRI. IEEE Trans. Med. Imaging **42**, 1707–1719 (2023)

Quantitative T2 Relaxometry in Fetal Brain: Validation Using Modified FaBiaN Fetal Brain MRI Simulator

Suryava Bhattacharya[1]([envelope]), Anthony Price[1,2,3], Alena Uus[1,3], Helena S. Sousa[1], Massimo Marenzana[2,3], Kathleen Colford[2,3], Peter Murkin[2,3], Maggie Lee[2,3], Lucilio Cordero-Grande[3,4], Rui Pedro Azeredo Gomes Teixeira[1,3], Shaihan J. Malik[1,3], and Maria Deprez[1,3]

[1] School of Biomedical Engineering and Imaging Sciences, King's College London, London, UK
suryava.bhattacharya@kcl.ac.uk
[2] Guy's and St Thomas Trust, London, UK
[3] Centre for the Developing Brain, King's College London, London, UK
[4] Biomedical Image Technologies, ETSI Telecomunicación, Universidad Politécnica de Madrid and CIBER-BBN, Madrid, Spain

Abstract. With development of fast imaging techniques and powerful motion correcting reconstruction techniques, high resolution 3D fetal brain images with a high level of anatomical detail are possible to acquire. A quantitative framework has been proposed that leverages fast imaging techniques and motion correcting reconstruction techniques to build quantitative T2 maps of the fetal brain. This study proposes a simulated phantom that modifies the FaBiaN fetal MRI simulated phantom to enable validation of this quantitative framework. We found that the slice-to-volume reconstruction (SVR) algorithm preserves quantitative T2 measurements and, therefore the proposed pipeline is suitable for reconstruction of quantitative T2 maps of fetal brain tissue.

Keywords: Fetal brain MRI · Relaxometry · Slice to volume registration

1 Introduction

The fetal period is characterised by rapid growth and, in the fetal brain, myelination, generation of synapses, movement of cells and changes in water result in observable changes in tissue properties. In addition, changes due to pathology may impacts fetal and post-natal development [14]. Relaxometry describes tissue relaxation properties in MRI [4] and therefore presents an opportunity to study fetal brain development and pathology. Traditional quantitative MRI methods, though, have been highly susceptible to motion, while requiring long scan times [13,20]. In the fetal setting, this presents a challenge, as relaxometry measurements will be corrupted by fetal motion and maternal breathing.

S. J. Malik and M. Deprez—Contributed equally.

D. Link-Sourani et al. (Eds.): PIPPI 2023, LNCS 14246, pp. 39–49, 2023.
https://doi.org/10.1007/978-3-031-45544-5_4

Related Work: Clinical fetal imaging relies on rapid sequences such as Single-shot turbo spin-echo (TSE) to avoid in-plane motion [9] and advances in motion correction have allowed for high quality 3D imaging of fetal brains [6] and other fetal anatomy [18,19]. Recently, echo planar imaging (EPI) has been leveraged to obtain T2* measurements in fetal brain [3,20] and other fetal tissues [1,15]. However, due to a lack of ground truth the quantitative fetal MRI measurements are difficult to validate. A recently developed simulated fetal brain MRI phantom, known as the Fetal Brain magnetic resonance Acquisition Numerical phantom (FaBiAN) [8], can facilitate such validation. This phantom integrates accurate simulations of signals from Siemens' Half-Fourier Acquisition Single-shot Turbo spin Echo (HASTE) sequence, also called Single-Shot Fast Spin Echo (SS-FSE for GE Healthcare), with different levels of fetal motion to simulate realistic fetal brain scans based on spatiotemporal fetal brain atlas [5].

Contributions: We propose a new framework to measure T2 relaxation time in the fetal brain by combining Single-shot TSE acquisition with varying echo times (TE) and SVR [6], using the SVR toolkit (SVRTK)[1]. We build on our previous work [2], in which we successfully validated our T2 measurement against a gold standard multi-echo spin-echo (MESE) sequence by scanning a phantom made up of a spherical flask of agar gel and five vials of MnCl2. However, a validation of such measurement for the motion corrupted fetal data has not been carried out thus far. To address this gap we propose a modified FaBiAN simulator which accurately models fetal acquisition of the Philip's system, on which we performed our fetal brain T2 measurements using five real fetal MRI datasets. Subsequently, we simulate realistic motion corrupted fetal data and quantify the measurement errors in reconstructed T2 maps to validate the SVR step in the T2 relaxometry framework for the fetal brain. Finally, we present measurements of T2 on five real fetal subjects using the validated framework.

2   Methodology

2.1   Quantitative T2 Measurement Framework for Fetal MRI

The proposed T2 relaxometry framework, validated against a gold-standard method for a static phantom in our previous work [2], is summarised in Fig. 1. The steps of this framework are:

1. Stacks are acquired in three approximately orthogonal views for three different TE = 80, 180 and 400 ms (a total of nine stacks) and denoised using a shearlet-based algorithm [7]. A selected stack, used in the reconstruction of the template volume, is manually brain-masked.
2. The fetal brain MRI for each TE is reconstructed separately using SVR with default parameters [6] on the three stacks of each TE. The reconstructed TE = 180 ms volume was used as a template for the reconstruction of the other

---

[1] https://github.com/SVRTK/SVRTK.

volumes to maximise the consistency of the volumes for different echo times. The TE = 80 and 400 ms volumes were further registered to the TE = 180 ms volume, and the entire set is registered to the fetal atlas for the given gestational age [17].

3. Using a pre-calculated dictionary of slice corrected SS-FSE signals, the T2 value for each voxel is found as the dictionary entry with a minimum scalar product with normalised measured signal.

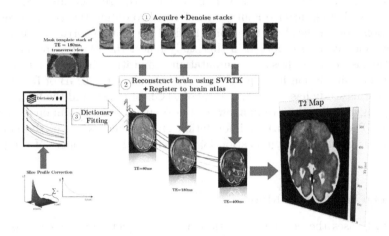

Fig. 1. The quantitative T2 measurement framework for fetal brain MRI.

This framework was applied to real fetal MRI data to obtain measurements of T2 in the fetal brain. To validate that the SVR step of the proposed framework preserves T2 measurements, we modified the FaBiAN phantom to generate simulated motion-corrupted fetal data from a simulated ground truth quantitative T2 maps of fetal brain, and applied the framework to measure the reconstruction error in the simulated T2 maps.

2.2   Overview of the FaBiAN Phantom

The FaBiAN phantom uses high resolution 3D fetal atlas segmentations [5] at 0.8 mm isotropic as the reference for its simulations. These segmentations are split into three tissue classes: white matter (WM), grey matter (GM) and cerebrospinal-fluid (CSF) with corresponding T1 and T2 values chosen by the authors [8]. The reference 3D segmentation map is then upsampled (using nearest-neighbour or NN) in the slice-select direction as a Gaussian slice profile is applied to the signals.

Signals are generated at each point on the upsampled reference map based on the tissue class of the given point resulting in a large matrix of signals for each point of the reference maps. Slices are then sampled based on the sampling scheme. Five percent of the slices were initially chosen, randomly, to have motion applied to them and before these slices are sampled, the upsampled reference map is translated and rotated to simulate motion and the signal matrix is updated with the signals based on the transformed reference map.

The slices are sampled by multiplying a Gaussian profile with the signals at the point of the given slice and summing across the slice-select direction to obtain the 2D slice. This is then transformed into a 2D k-space representation of the slice using MATLAB's fast Fourier transform and this k-space is sampled based on HASTE (Siemen's) or SSTSE (GE Healthcare) and any acceleration factors. This is then inverse Fourier transformed to obtain the 2D slice and the this is done for all the slices to obtain the final 3D motion corrupted image.

The modifications proposed in this study reflect the Philip's specific implementation as well as address the computational limitations imposed in this study. The original simulation had up to "16 CPU workers with 20 GB of RAM each" [8], while this study has access to a total of 64 GB of RAM (and the final modifications suggested in this study allow for the simulations to be ran on a machine with 16 GB of RAM). Further information on implementation of the FaBiAN phantom is given in the publication [8] written by the developers of the phantom.

2.3   The Fetal Brain Model

This study uses the normative spatiotemporal magnetic resonance atlas [5] in our simulations and reference T1 and T2 values identical to the original FaBiAN phantom [8]. Our initial real fetal brain T2 measurements [2] confirmed that these values (232 ms for WM and 162 for GM) are realistic and there are no literature T1 values for fetal brains at the time of this study.

2.4   Modelling Fetal Motion

Fetal motion was modelled in the FaBiAN phantom using motion randomly sampled from an uniform distribution at 3 different levels with each level corresponding to an amplitude of 3D translation and 3D rotation in any direction in 3D space. The developers of the FaBiAN phantom took clinical advise to inform their model of fetal motion [8] and, as such, this study closely follows their motion models while proposing slight modifications.

This study applies the light motion and moderate motion amplitudes from the FaBiAN phantom, which are defined as $[-1, 1]$ mm and $[-3, 3]$ mm maximum translation in any direction in 3D space, and $[-2, 2]°$ and $[-5, 5]°$ maximum rotation along an axis represented by an arbitrary 3D vector in 3D space [8]. These are for each incidence of motion. However in this study, the translation displacements and rotation angles were obtained using a normal distribution with the amplitudes representing $3 \times \sigma$ of the normal distribution. The rotation axes were chosen by an uniform distribution, as in the original FaBiAN phantom.

In a similar manner to the FaBiAN phantom, this study also translates and rotates the fetal atlas before sampling the slice and uses this transformed atlas as the new reference. However, in this study there is a 10% (for light motion) or 12.5% (for moderate motion) chance of a transformation being made to the atlas before sampling. The slices during the sampling of which a transformation is applied is not pre-selected (as these slices are randomly pre-selected in the original FaBiAN phantom).

In addition, transformations in the FaBiAN phantom were interpolated using nearest neighbour interpolation [8]. In contrast, we are using linear interpolation on individual tissue classes and max-voting to transform the segmentations in order to preserve image quality. We implement interleaved slice order with four packages, according to our Philips acquisition slice order, (i.e. 1,5,9... then 2,6,10..., then 3,7,11,... and finally 4,8,12,...) instead of the Siemens' interleaved scheme.

2.5   Modelling Signals with Slice Profiles

Although pure T2 relaxation can be modelled as a simple exponential decay, in practice the use of non-180° refocusing pulses, and slice selective pulses in general, leads to signals deviating from this relationship and, thus we use the EPG formalism [11, 12, 21] to model this extra complexity.

In addition, signals are influenced by the varying flip angles along the slice profile as the slice profile is not an ideal square. To model these flip angles, refocusing and excitation pulses from the Philip's scanners are utilised and the overall signal for the given T2 entry of the dictionary is modelled by integrating the signal along each point on the slice profile [10].

We proposed an optimised simulation of MRI signals in individual slices, which deviates from the original FaBiaN implementation. First, the slice position is calculated based on the slice index and resolution in the slice direction. A generous window is applied in the slice direction (approximately 6× the slice width) to fully capture the entire slice profile and any off-centre signal. All the T1 and T2 values in this window of the reference map are obtained. This is then upsampled based on the number of points (experimentally set to 62) on the slice profile being simulated. The signals are then modelled at each of these points based on the flip angle profile and local T1 and T2 values, and the final signal decay (a signal as a function of time) is calculated by summing along the slice profile direction, resulting in 2D + t slice object. The entire unsampled k-space for this slice is then obtained through a Fourier transform of this profile across each time point.

2.6   Sampling K-Space

For Single-shot TSE images, slightly more than half of the k-space is sampled to speed up acquisition (controlled by partial Fourier factor parameter) and the rest of the k-space is zero-filled. We propose to manipulate the TE by changing the partial Fourier factor, such that the centre of k-space is sampled at the given TE.

To further speed up acquisition, Philips uses SENSE to reduce acquired field of view (similarly to GRAPPA in the Siemens [8]) and this study simulates a pseudo SENSE (factor 2) reconstruction by sampling two lines of k-space for each echo. Complex noise is added to k-space before inverse Fourier transforming to image space to get the final slice image. We do not model any field inhomogeneities in these simulations.

2.7   Modelling the Signals for the Dictionary

The dictionary signals were modelled both in this and our previous work [2] in a similar manner to that described in Sect. 2.5. Except the T2 was constant for across all slice points (as the dictionary has no spatial information and, therefore it cannot be known how T2 might vary across the slice), based on the T2 entry of the dictionary for which the signal is being modelled. As such, partial volume is not modelled but the effect on the signal due to a finite signal profile is modelled. The T1 value for the entire dictionary is kept constant at $T1 = 3000$ ms. In addition, the resolution of the dictionary across the T2 values is 1ms and the range of T2s in the dictionary are from 25–3000 ms (as upon experimentation, T2 in the range of 0–25 ms was not required to be measured and these dictionary entries produced unreliable results due to the rapid decay).

2.8   Simulated Experiments

We apply the quantitative T2 measurement framework (Sect. 2.1, [2]) to reconstruct reference fetal brain MRI T2 maps (Sect. 2.3) from the simulated fetal data generated using our modified FaBiaN simulator. The simulated data contains three stacks with orthogonal orientation per TE, with in-plane resolution 1.25 mm, slice thickness 2.5 mm and slice spacing 1.25 mm (overlapping slices). We achieve TE = 80, 180 and 400 ms by using partial fourier factors 0.6, 0.8 and 0.96 respectively.

We consider five different settings in our experiments:

1. We do not model any fetal motion or partial volume (PV) along the slice profile. This ideal scenario allows us to exclude the SVR step as it presents artifacts only created through k-space sampling and not due to the slice-profile effects and therefore does not require any motion correction or super-resolution (SR) reconstruction.
2. We model PV along the slice profile but model no motion and do not implement any SR or SVR reconstruction.
3. We model PV along the slice profile but model no motion. We apply SR reconstruction and only global rigid stack alignment by using a single SVR iteration.
4. We model the entire motion simulation (with PV and motion) with light motion and apply SVR to reconstruct the T2 maps.

5. We model the entire motion simulation (with PV and motion) with moderate motion and apply SVR to reconstruct the T2 maps.

These experiments are done for fetal phantoms with gestational ages 21, 27, 29, 31, 35 weeks from the spatiotemporal atlas to simulate the same ages as those scanned in the quantitative framework.

2.9   Fetal Brain Measurements

The quantitative fetal scans were acquired on a Philip's INGENIA 1.5T scanner in clinical sessions with consent to research. Five subjects were imaged, with fetal anomalies as commented by radiologists. Single-shot TSE images were acquired with in-plane resolution 1.25 mm, slice thickness 2.5 mm and slice spacing 1.25 mm, and TE = 80, 180 and 400 ms (as described in Fig. 1) in three diverse views per TE (resulting in nine stacks per subject). Due to the tight fit of the FOV and the maternal body, the views were not perfectly orthogonal to avoid wrap artefacts. However, the views were sufficiently diverse to allow for successful SVR. The scan calibration was performed only once to ensure consistency. The T2 maps were reconstructed according the pipeline presented in Sect. 2.1.

3   Results

3.1   Simulated Fetal MRI

Figure 2 presents different views for an example of images generated from the simulation of motion for GA = 29 weeks. These demonstrate a distinct difference in the levels of motion.

3.2   Reconstruction of T2 Maps from Simulated Fetal Data

Quantitative Evaluation: Figure 3 presents the errors between original and reconstructed phantom T2 maps across all gestational ages. The box and whisker plots show median and inter-quartile range (IQR) of the errors in ms, and demonstrate the trend of the errors across five different experiments. The plot demonstrates small median errors in white matter (−2.7 ms, −3.8 ms, −1.5 ms, −2.0 ms and −2.5 ms for the experiments 1–5, respectively), suggesting a minimal bias in the measurement. The IQR of the errors stay consistent in the WM. In experiment 1 the quartiles range from −12 ms to 6 ms, whereas in experiment 5 these range from −13 to 7 ms. However, these ranges are still relatively small (less then 10%) compared to the nominal WM T2 of 232 ms. However, in the grey matter errors are larger, resulting from significant partial volume effects affecting the thin fetal cortex. Median errors show positive bias, consistent with shorter cortical T2 being mixed with longer T2 of white matter and cerebro-spinal fluid (CSF). Notably, the SR reconstruction diminishes the bias and reduces the spread of errors in the cortex, especially in the scenario of PV and no motion with SR reconstruction, or experiment 3, in comparison

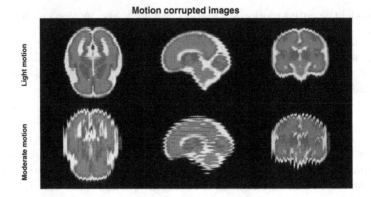

Fig. 2. The result of the motion artifacts simulated based on fetal motion and the slice and k-space sampling mentioned above.

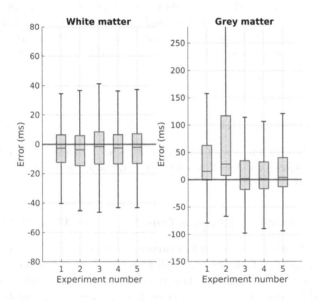

Fig. 3. Boxplots summarising the errors in ms of all the experiments (1–5) given above and amalgamated across all the simulations across all gestational ages.

to experiment 2 (PV, no motion, no SR reconstruction). While in experiment 1, the Quartiles range from 0 ms to 63 ms, in experiment 3 the Quartiles range from −18 ms to 35 ms with the lowest median error of 1.6 ms. Moderate motion introduced marginally greater error in cortex in terms of bias and spread, however this was lower than experiment 2, which models partial volume but has no SR or SVR reconstruction.

Qualitative Evaluation: Example reconstructed T2 maps for each experiment are presented in Fig. 4. We can observe that SR reconstruction (experiments 3–5) results in better delineation of the cortex. In particular in experiment 3 with no motion, it can be seen that the cortex has been most accurately recovered by SR. The percentage error maps demonstrate, that the errors are dominated by partial volume effects, especially on the boundary with CSF.

3.3   Fetal Measurements

Table 1 presents average T2 measurements for different brain tissue types obtained from quantitative MRI scans of five fetal subjects. We observe that T2 values are consistently higher for fetuses in comparison to neonates. Fetal T2 values are also consistently higher in comparison to fetal T2* values across all tissue types. The values in Table 1 were obtained as an average across all fetal subjects.

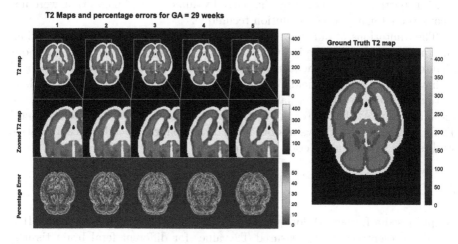

Fig. 4. The T2 maps (top row), highlight of the separation of cortex and white matter (middle row) and absolute percentage difference bottom row and the ground truth T2 map is given on the right. The T2 values were obtained based on the scheme described in [8]

Table 1. Table comparing values of fetal T2 of this study to neonatal T2 and to fetal T2* in literature. The full table including the mean values over each ROI ($\pm\sigma$ over the ROI) for each subject is given in the Supplementary material.

Tissue	Average Fetal T2 (ms) $\pm\sigma$ (ms)	Neonatal T2 (ms) $\pm\sigma$ (ms) Using JSR [16] on 3T	Literature T2* (ms) $\pm\sigma$ (ms) Vasylechko [20] 1.5T	Literature T2* (ms) $\pm\sigma$ (ms) Blazejewska [3] 1.5T
Cortex	199 ± 33	133 ± 29	–	163 ± 30
DGM	201 ± 26	132 ± 45	Thalamus: 154 ± 24	–
WM	283 ± 39	218 ± 50	FWM: 234 ± 38	FWM: 259 ± 34
Subplate	292 ± 43	–	–	268 ± 17

4   Discussion

In this work we validated a framework for quantitative T2 measurement of fetal brain MRI [2] using a modified FaBiaN fetal brain MRI simulator. The results suggest that our proposed framework is accurate, with errors primarily driven by partial volume effects on tissue boundaries. We have shown that the SVR step preserves the T2 values. The median errors are very close to 0ms, proving that no bias is being introduced by the reconstructions. Inter-quartile ranges are within 10ms for WM showing good accuracy in homogeneous areas. The inter-quartile ranges are higher within the cortex, especially in positive direction, which is consistent with partial volume on boundaries with CSF. In addition, the reconstruction process recovers crucial structural details such as cortex which is particularly affected by the partial volume in the images that were not reconstructed using super-resolution technique.

The limitations of our modified phantom include lack of clinical validation, and further analysis of the individual elements of SVR pipeline. Currently, our phantom is specific to the acquisition parameters of our fetal MRI sequences, and we have not modelled the field inhomogeneities or signal drop-out due to in-plane motion. These present potential future works to further improve the physics of the simulation. At the time of this study, there are no other measurements of fetal T2 for comparison of the values obtained in this paper. Therefore, comparative studies may present a direction of future work.

5   Conclusion

We proposed a framework for quantitative T2 measurement of fetal brain MRI. We also presented initial measured T2 values for different fetal brain tissues. Our validation using a proposed modified FaBiaN simulator suggest feasibility of the our framework to study fetal brain and pathology.

Acknowledgements. This work was supported by the funding from the EPSRC Centre for Doctoral Training in Smart Medical Imaging (EP/S022104/1), the core funding from the Wellcome/EPSRC Centre for Medical Engineering [WT203148/Z/16/Z] and by the National Institute for Health Research Clinical Research Facility. The views expressed are those of the author(s) and not necessarily those of the NHS, the NIHR or the Department of Health and Social Care.

References

1. Avena-Zampieri, C.L., et al.: Assessment of normal pulmonary development using functional magnetic resonance imaging techniques. Am. J. Obstet. Gynecol. MFM 5(6), 100935 (2023)
2. Bhattacharya, S., et al.: In-vivo t2 measurements of fetal brain in 1.5t (2023). https://submissions.mirasmart.com/ISMRM2023/Itinerary/PresentationDetail. aspx?evdid=3165, iSMRM - Abstract 0273

3. Blazejewska, A.I., et al.: 3d in utero quantification of t2* relaxation times in human fetal brain tissues for age optimized structural and functional MRI. Magn. Reson. Med. **78**(3), 909–916 (2017)

4. Deoni, S.C., et al.: Mapping infant brain myelination with magnetic resonance imaging. J. Neurosci. **31**(2), 784–791 (2011)

5. Gholipour, A., et al.: A normative spatiotemporal MRI atlas of the fetal brain for automatic segmentation and analysis of early brain growth. Sci. Rep. **7**(1), 476 (2017)

6. Kuklisova-Murgasova, M., Quaghebeur, G., Rutherford, M.A., Hajnal, J.V., Schnabel, J.A.: Reconstruction of fetal brain MRI with intensity matching and complete outlier removal. Med. Image Anal. **16**(8), 1550–1564 (2012)

7. Kutyniok, G., Lemvig, J., Lim, W.Q.: Optimally sparse approximations of 3D functions by compactly supported shearlet frames. SIAM J. Math. Anal. **44**(4), 2962–3017 (2012)

8. Lajous, H., et al.: A fetal brain magnetic resonance acquisition numerical phantom (fabian). Sci. Rep. **12**(1), 8682 (2022)

9. Levine, D., Hatabu, H., Gaa, J., Atkinson, M.W., Edelman, R.: Fetal anatomy revealed with fast MR sequences. AJR Am. J. Roentgenol. **167**(4), 905–908 (1996)

10. Malik, S.J., Kenny, G.D., Hajnal, J.V.: Slice profile correction for transmit sensitivity mapping using actual flip angle imaging. Magn. Reson. Med. **65**(5), 1393–1399 (2011)

11. Malik, S.J., Teixeira, R.P.A., Hajnal, J.V.: Extended phase graph formalism for systems with magnetization transfer and exchange. Magn. Reson. Med. **80**(2), 767–779 (2018)

12. Malik, S.: mriphysics/epg-x: First public version (version v1. 0). Zenodo, 10–5281 (2017)

13. Péran, P., et al.: Voxel-based analysis of r2* maps in the healthy human brain. J. Magn. Reson. Imaging Off. J. Int. Soc. Magn. Reson. Med. **26**(6), 1413–1420 (2007)

14. Rutherford, M.A.: Magnetic resonance imaging of the fetal brain. Curr. Opin. Obstet. Gynecol. **21**(2), 180–186 (2009)

15. Sethi, S., et al.: Quantification of 1.5 t t1 and t2* relaxation times of fetal tissues in uncomplicated pregnancies. J. Magn. Reson. Imaging **54**(1), 113–121 (2021)

16. Teixeira, R.P.A., Malik, S.J., Hajnal, J.V.: Joint system relaxometry (JSR) and cramer-rao lower bound optimization of sequence parameters: a framework for enhanced precision of despot t1 and t2 estimation. Magn. Reson. Med. **79**(1), 234–245 (2018)

17. Uus, A., et al.: Spatio-temporal atlas of normal fetal craniofacial feature development and CNN-based ocular biometry for motion-corrected fetal MRI. In: Sudre, C.H., et al. (eds.) UNSURE/PIPPI -2021. LNCS, vol. 12959, pp. 168–178. Springer, Cham (2021). https://doi.org/10.1007/978-3-030-87735-4_16

18. Uus, A., et al.: Deformable slice-to-volume registration for reconstruction of quantitative T2* placental and fetal MRI. In: Hu, Y., et al. (eds.) ASMUS/PIPPI -2020. LNCS, vol. 12437, pp. 222–232. Springer, Cham (2020). https://doi.org/10.1007/978-3-030-60334-2_22

19. Uus, A., et al.: Deformable slice-to-volume registration for motion correction of fetal body and placenta MRI. IEEE Trans. Med. Imaging **39**(9), 2750–2759 (2020)

20. Vasylechko, S., et al.: T2* relaxometry of fetal brain at 1.5 tesla using a motion tolerant method. Magn. Reson. Med. **73**(5), 1795–1802 (2015)

21. Weigel, M.: Extended phase graphs: dephasing, rf pulses, and echoes-pure and simple. J. Magn. Reson. Imaging **41**(2), 266–295 (2015)

Fetal Cardiac Image Analysis

Towards Automatic Risk Prediction of Coarctation of the Aorta from Fetal CMR Using Atlas-Based Segmentation and Statistical Shape Modelling

Paula Ramirez[✉], Uxio Hermida[✉], Alena Uus, Milou P. M. van Poppel,
Irina Grigorescu, Johannes K. Steinweg, David F. A. Lloyd,
Kuberan Pushparajah, Adelaide de Vecchi, Andrew King, Pablo Lamata,
and Maria Deprez

School of Biomedical Engineering and Imaging Sciences, King's College London,
London, UK
{paula.ramirez_gilliland,uxio.hermida_nunez}@kcl.ac.uk

Abstract. This paper proposes a fully-automated technique for estimation of an antenatal risk score for Coarctation of the Aorta (CoA) from fetal T2-weighted 3D cardiac magnetic resonance imaging (CMR). Our framework combines automated multi-class fetal cardiac vessel segmentation based on two fully-labelled atlases (control and CoA) with statistical shape analysis of the fetal arch. The segmentation framework is weakly-supervised, requiring only condition-specific atlas labels which are propagated to training subjects. The proposed shape analysis method utilizes the predicted segmentation to extract a set of centerlines and radii capturing the shape of the fetal arch. Principal Component Analysis (PCA) and Linear Discriminant Analysis (LDA) are then applied to derive a CoA risk score. The segmentation framework achieves a mean Dice of 0.86 ± 0.03 for the aortic region. The CoA shape biomarker accurately discriminated between false positives (FP) and CoA cases (AUC 0.93) and showed good generalisability in an independent test set (AUC 0.87), achieving comparable performance to approaches using manual segmentations. Our proposed fully-automatic technique has the potential to improve the antenatal diagnosis of CoA from 3D fetal CMR data.

Keywords: Fetal CMR · Suspected Coarctation of the Aorta · Shape Analysis · Vessel Segmentation · Fetal Atlas · Weakly-supervised learning

1 Introduction

Coarctation of the Aorta (CoA) is a congenital heart defect characterized by the narrowing of the aortic isthmus after the postnatal closure of the arterial duct (AD). CoA accounts for 6–8% of patients with Congenital Heart Disease (CHD),

---

P. Ramirez and U. Hermida—The first two authors contributed equally.

© The Author(s), under exclusive license to Springer Nature Switzerland AG 2023
D. Link-Sourani et al. (Eds.): PIPPI 2023, LNCS 14246, pp. 53–63, 2023.
https://doi.org/10.1007/978-3-031-45544-5_5

and up to 0.06–0.08% of the general population [8]. Antenatal diagnosis of CoA is challenging, with high false-positive rates of up to 80% [2].

Recent advancements in acquisition and reconstruction techniques [14] have demonstrated the added value of motion-corrected 3D fetal cardiac magnetic resonance imaging (CMR) for vascular visualization as an adjunct to echocardiography [9,10].

Recent studies have shown the potential of utilizing shape biomarkers derived from 3D fetal CMR acquisitions to enhance the antenatal diagnsosi of CoA [4,10]. The extraction of these shape biomarkers currently relies on semi-automatic frameworks that require time-consuming manual input from clinical experts. Additionally, semi-automatic pipelines are subject to inter- and intra-observer variability. Consequently, there is a need for a fully-automatic technique capable of extracting the characteristic shape signature in CoA from fetal 3D CMR data.

1.1 Contributions

Our work proposes a fully-automated technique that employs joint registration and segmentation training for weakly-supervised multi-class vessel segmentation, requiring only fully-labelled atlases during training, and no labels for inference. We then utilise these predictions for fetal arch shape analysis and shape biomarker extraction. This is the first fully-automated prenatal risk score analysis framework for suspected CoA using novel fetal 3D CMR data.

2 Methods

2.1 Dataset Description

The dataset comprises T2w 3D black-blood CMR reconstructions. This includes 57 healthy control cases (median gestational age (GA): 30.5 weeks; interquartile range: 29.7–31.9) and 150 cases with suspected CoA, out of which 48 were true confirmed CoA cases (median GA: 32.0 weeks; interquartile range: 30.9–33.4) and 102 were FPs (median GA: 31.9 weeks; interquartile range: 30.9–32.9). Data were acquired at Evelina London Children's Hospital with a 1.5 T Ingenia MR system. The acquisition sequence used is T2-weighted SSFSE sequence (TR = 20,000 ms, TE = 50 ms, FA = 90°, voxel size = 1.25 × 1.25 mm, slice thickness = 2.5 mm and slice overlap = 1.25 mm). The raw datasets comprised 2D images of 6–12 multi-slice stacks, encompassing the fetal thorax in three orthogonal planes. All research participants provided written informed consent.

The 2D stacks were reconstructed into 3D volumes with Slice-to-Volume Registration (SVR) [6,7] and Deformable SVR [14,15] (DSVR, higher quality) to 0.75 mm isotropic resolution. In addition, the dataset includes two fully-labelled atlases[1] [16], one for controls and one for CoA/FPs (see Fig. 1).

---

[1] https://gin.g-node.org/SVRTK/.

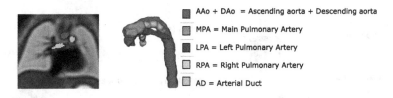

Fig. 1. Illustration of our healthy atlas with multi-class vessels.

Data Preprocessing: For the label propagation framework, fetal T2-weighted 3D images were affinely registered via classical registration[2] to the pertinent atlas in each case, using the diagnosis as a prior for atlas selection. All cases were cropped to a standardised cardiac vessel region. The dataset was split into training and validation (N = 164, controls = 51, FP = 64, CoA = 40), and test sets (N = 52, controls = 6, FP = 38, CoA = 8). Fetal CMR image intensities were rescaled between 0 and 1 prior to segmentation training.

2.2   Automated Segmentation

Joint segmentation and registration training [18] has been proposed for semi-supervised learning, reporting synergistic network improvements. One-shot segmentation techniques for synthetic data augmentation [19] have also been successfully applied in a semi-supervised segmentation setting. Atlas-based label propagation (LP) consists of transferring labelling information from fully-labelled anatomical atlases to individual subjects via image registration. This technique has been successfully applied to segment multi-class vascular structures in T2w 3D fetal CMR images [12], showing good generalisability to distinct aortic arch anomalies.

Our strategy builds on existing training approaches [12,18]. Using the prior information of the diagnosis, the pertinent atlas is selected (healthy or CoA) for each subject. We register the CoA atlas to all cases with suspected CoA (i.e., FP and CoA). The proposed segmentation framework is illustrated in Fig. 2. This is composed of (1) atlas-based LP using VoxelMorph [1]; and (2) Attention U-Net [11] segmentation. The segmentation training strategy follows four steps, where the output of one network (LP or Attention U-Net) is used to supervise the other network, similar to [18]. The training steps are described below.

(1) Unsupervised LP: The pre-trained VoxelMorph LP network proposed in [12][3] is used to generate initial training labels, by propagating the multi-class atlas labels to each subject space. **(2) Init Attention U-Net**: An Attention U-Net is trained using these labels for vessel segmentation. **(3) Supervised LP**: LP is retrained using an auxiliary segmentation loss to improve label accuracy. This loss incorporates Attention U-Net predictions (keeping Attention U-Net weights frozen) and warped atlas labels. The term *supervised* in this context

---

[2] https://github.com/BioMedIA/MIRTK.

[3] https://github.com/SVRTK/.

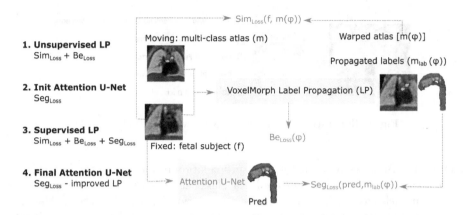

Fig. 2. Proposed segmentation framework. LP generates training labels, which are used by Attention U-Net. LP is then enhanced via supervised training, with a Final Attention U-Net trained on these improved labels. ϕ = displacement field.

refers to the inclusion of segmentation information, not any human intervention. **(4) Final Attention U-Net**: Attention U-Net is retrained on the improved propagated labels (keeping LP weights frozen), with the Tversky (TK) Loss loss function. Our motivation for following this four-step training strategy is to automatically generate accurate training labels for Attention U-Net, considering the absence of ground truth training labels. Although LP is in itself a segmentation strategy, it is highly dependent on optimal affine alignment between atlas and fetal subjects. Attention U-Net learns from both intensity and spatial information, resulting in a more generalisable framework, especially for cases with strong anatomical deviations from the atlases. Note that atlases are only required at training time, during inference the prediction is done by **Final Attention U-Net solely**. A quality control inspection of the initial propagated training labels was conducted.

Label Propagation: The similarity loss function (Sim_{Loss}) is Local Normalised Cross Correlation (LNCC) [1]. Bending energy loss (Be_{Loss}) regularises the displacement field [3], with a weight of 0.2. A dice loss (Seg_{Loss}) is used for supervised LP training, with a weight of 50 (as the aim is accurate label propagation). A five-layer U-Net-based architecture is used for LP, with blocks of 3D strided convolutions with leaky ReLU activations.

CNN Segmentation: A 3D five-layer Attention U-Net is employed [11][4] with output channels = 32, 64, 128, 256 and 512, convolution and upsampling kernel size of 3, ReLU activation, and dropout = 0.2. Our final segmenter uses the TK Loss [13] to reduce the risk of topologically inconsistent segmentations with

---

[4] https://github.com/Project-MONAI/MONAI/.,.

disconnected vessels. We used a FN weight of $\beta = 0.6$ and a FP weight of $\alpha = 0.4$. Loss weights were empirically selected via hyperparameter tuning.

Training: The networks are trained until convergence (NVIDIA GeForce RTX 3090 GPU), with linearly decaying learning rates initialised at 5×10^{-4} (LP) and 1×10^{-3} (Attention U-Net) and an AdamW optimiser for segmenter training, based on validation set hyperparameter tuning. Project MONAI spatial and intensity data augmentation are employed (random intensity shifts, Gaussian Smoothing and Noise, contrast adjustments and bias fields, and affine deformations).

2.3   Statistical Shape Analysis

Shape Encoding: The fetal arch shape can be encoded by a set of centerline points and their captured radius. Previous methods for analyzing the fetal arch shape have required a manual selection of landmarks to extract the centerlines [4]. In this study, we modified that approach to enable the fully-automatic encoding of shapes without user involvement. Initially, a set of landmarks was automatically detected using the network's multi-class predictions. These landmarks include: 1. The endpoint of the descending aorta (DAo); 2. The center of mass of the main pulmonary artery (MPA); 3. The center of mass of the arterial duct (AD); 4. The starting point of the ascending aorta (AAo). The multi-class predictions were then converted into a single-label 3D model to ensure smooth shape transitions between labels for shape encoding. Subsequently, two sets of centerlines were extracted separately. Firstly, the centerline from landmark 1 (DAo) to landmark 2 (MPA) was extracted. Then, landmark 3 (AD) was used to clip the 3D model and facilitate accurate centerline extraction using landmarks 1 (DAo) and 4 (AAo). Following the extraction of centerlines and the geometrical decomposition of the bifurcation, the individual centerlines were merged into a single centerline. Each anatomical segment was then resampled to a predetermined number of points: 25 points for AAo and MPA, and 50 points for DAo. Finally, the centerlines were aligned in a common reference space using the bifurcation origin, the direction from the bifurcation to the MPA, and the vertical direction of the DAo. Once the centerlines are obtained, Principal Component Analysis (PCA) can be applied to construct a statistical shape model that captures the most common variations in shape within the cohort [4]. All features were standardized before performing PCA.

CoA Risk Score: Fisher Linear Discriminant Analysis (LDA) is used to find the optimal anatomical linear axis that best discriminates between confirmed CoA and FP cases [17]. PCA modes capturing up to 90% of the shape variability in the population were included. Along the LDA axis, each anatomy is characterized by a single score (referred to as the CoA risk score). The discriminative performance of this risk score was assessed with the area under the receiver operating characteristic (AUC) and tested in resubstitution (RS) and leave-one-out cross-validation (LOOCV) to assess for overfitting. The performance was assessed on the independent test set to study the risk score generalisability.

3 Results

3.1 Segmentation

Quantitative Analysis: Segmentation predictions are compared against manually corrected propagated label segmentations (GT) for 16 unseen test set cases. Table 1 displays vessel dice scores comparing the two CNN segmentation steps.

Table 1. Vessel dice scores (standard deviation) on unseen test cases.

Experiment	Aorta	MPA	LPA	RPA	AD
Final Attention U-Net	**0.86 (0.03)**	0.82 (0.08)	**0.76 (0.09)**	**0.78 (0.07)**	0.82 (0.05)
Init Attention U-Net	0.85 (0.04)	**0.84 (0.06)**	0.74 (0.09)	0.77 (0.07)	**0.83 (0.06)**

The final framework generally achieves higher scores, however, these are not statistically significant by a Mann-Whitney U test. Nonetheless, we observe a reduction in the number of lower-scoring outliers, particularly for the whole vessels region of interest (ROI, binary joined labels) and for the aorta (DAo + AAo) by retraining the network on improved labels (**Final Attention U-Net**). This is captured in Fig. 3 (higher ASD and HD95 in **Init Attention U-Net**). Achieving optimal performance in the aortic region is crucial, as shape metrics are extracted specifically from this region.

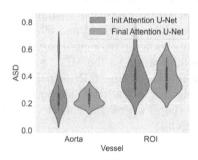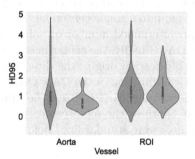

Fig. 3. Average surface distance (ASD) and 95th percentile of the Hausdorff distance (HD95) metrics (mm, lower = better). Aorta = AAo + DAo. This depicts the improvements over including our four-step training approach, using the output of one network to improve the next.

Visual Inspection: Figure 4 displays visual evidence of the improved LP results, achieved by retraining the LP technique using **Initial Attention U-Net** predictions. The proposed framework incorporates an additional CNN, trained on the refined LP (**Final Attention U-Net**), reducing the dependency on accurate affine alignment and anatomical similarity to the atlas, a persistent issue in LP. Figure 5 showcases a registration failure, where part of the aorta and AD are predicted in an erroneous location, due to the reasons referenced above. Contrastingly, **Final Attention U-Net** generalises well to this case.

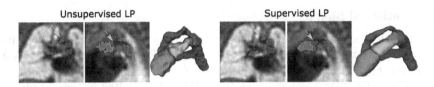

Fig. 4. Label propagation test set predictions before and after supervision. Yellow arrows indicate improvements observed in **Supervised LP** (Color figure online).

An additional comparative evaluation is carried out, to assess the advantages of **Final Attention U-Net** over label propagation (**Supervised LP**). This involved a manual inspection and prediction scoring of 52 unseen test cases. The scoring system ranges from 1 to 3, where a **score of 1** denotes accurate aortic vessel delineation, a **score of 2** indicates partial errors such as slight over or under-segmentation of the aorta, and a **score of 3** indicates complete misplacement of the segmented aortic region (see Fig. 5 for an example). Table 2 displays the superiority of **Final Attention U-Net** over **Supervised LP**.

Table 2. Number of cases for the qualitative assessment (1→3 = best→worst).

	Score 1	Score 2	Score 3
Final Attention U-Net	45	7	0
Supervised LP	25	11	17

Quality Control: Nine (out of 164) cases were excluded from the statistical shape analysis due to segmentation issues. These cases presented segmentation errors and imprecisions including vessel merging, erroneous or unclear insertion point between the aortic isthmus and AD/DAo bifurcation, extreme vessel thinnings and vessel splittings. Some of these issues were due to low image quality, and/or considerable anatomical variations to the atlases such as bilateral superior vena cava (SVC).

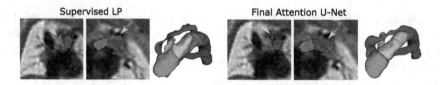

Fig. 5. Yellow arrows signal misregistration errors resulting in erroneously segmented vessel regions (qualitative score = 3). Attention U-Net corrects this. (Color figure online)

3.2 Statistical Shape Analysis

The statistical shape model was constructed using 155 cases with successful network segmentations, including 51 controls, 40 FP and 64 confirmed CoA cases. The first 14 PCA modes captured 90% of the shape variability in the population. Their linear combination (i.e. LDA axis) resulted in a discriminant score (i.e. CoA risk score) able to classify between FP and CoA cases with an AUC of 0.93 in resubstitution, comparable to existing frameworks trained on manual segmentations (AUC = 0.943) [4]. The model showed small overfitting in LOOCV, dropping to 0.88. The mean CoA risk scores along the LDA axis were as follows: 1.31 ± 0.69 for confirmed CoA cases, -0.15 ± 0.66 for FP, and -0.83 ± 0.59 for the control population. Furthermore, the CoA risk score demonstrated good generalisability when assessed on the independent test set, achieving an AUC of 0.87 for distinguishing between FP and CoA cases. The mean CoA risk scores along the LDA axis were: 0.88 ± 0.64 for CoA cases, -0.28 ± 0.77 for FP, and -0.97 ± 0.54 for controls.

Figure 6 shows the extreme phenotypes along the LDA axis corresponding to the healthy and CoA populations. The discriminant axis captured shape features such as great artery asymmetry, variation in the angle at which the aortic isthmus inserts in the bifurcation, the proximal displacement of the aortic isthmus, and the course of the AD inserting into the aortic arch.

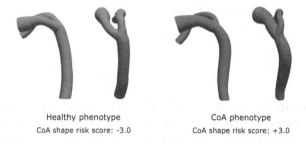

Healthy phenotype
CoA shape risk score: -3.0

CoA phenotype
CoA shape risk score: +3.0

Fig. 6. Extreme phenotypes resulting from the optimal linear discriminant analysis (LDA) to distinguish between false positive (FP) and confirmed coarctation of the aorta (CoA) cases.

4 Discussion

The present study proposes an end-to-end fully automated CoA risk score classification strategy for fetal CMR. We achieve comparable performance to existing manual frameworks, requiring solely labelled atlases during training. Our work has strong clinical application in aiding the discernment of true CoA cases.

We achieve weakly-supervised segmentation, displaying promising results for aortic arch segmentation. Supervising both registration and segmentation networks with the predicted labels improves the overall segmentation performance, particularly in the correctness of the aortic arch contouring.

The CoA risk score built from automatic segmentations showed comparable performance to previously reported models trained on manual segmentations [4,5]. Notably, the automatic LDA axis captured shape features such as the proximal displacement of the aortic isthmus, variations in the angle of aortic isthmus insertion on the bifurcation, and relative vessel size between the AD and the aortic isthmus. These features have been previously identified as relevant shape features in the prediction of CoA [4,10]. However, it is important to note that some discrepancies between our LDA extreme phenotypes and those reported in previous work were observed. These discrepancies may arise due to potential biases introduced by either observers and their manual segmentation or the automatic segmentation process. Further investigation is warranted to understand the impact of segmentation styles in the derivation of the CoA risk score and the mechanistic interpretations of the role of shape in the pathophysiology of CoA.

Future work should explore the impact of the empirical selection of the TK loss weights in the network predictions, the CoA risk score and the associated extreme phenotypes. Additionally, an investigation into excluded segmentation cases due to topological errors is required, which could lead to the development of an automated segmentation quality control system.

5 Conclusion

We have presented a fully-automatic framework to extract a shape biomarker capturing the shape signature in CoA (i.e. CoA risk score) from motion-corrected T2w 3D black-blood CMR reconstructions. Our work has the potential to aid antenatal diagnosis of CoA.

Acknowledgements. We would like to acknowledge funding from the EPSRC Centre for Doctoral Training in Smart Medical Imaging (EP/S022104/1).

We thank everyone who was involved in the acquisition and examination of the datasets and all participating mothers. This work was supported by the Rosetrees Trust [A2725], the Wellcome/EPSRC Centre for Medical Engineering at King's College London [WT 203148/Z/16/Z], the Wellcome Trust and EPSRC IEH award [102431] for the iFIND project, the NIHR Clinical Research Facility (CRF) at Guy's and St Thomas' and by the National Institute for Health Research Biomedical Research Centre based at Guy's and St Thomas' NHS Foundation Trust and King's College London.

The views expressed are those of the authors and not necessarily those of the NHS, the NIHR or the Department of Health.

All fetal MRI datasets used in this work were processed subject to informed consent of the participants [REC: 07/H0707/105; REC: 14/LO/1806].

The work follows appropriate ethical standards in conducting research and writing the manuscript, following all applicable laws and regulations regarding treatment of animals or human subjects.

References

1. Balakrishnan, G., Zhao, A., Sabuncu, M.R., Guttag, J., Dalca, A.V.: Voxelmorph: a learning framework for deformable medical image registration. IEEE Trans. Med. Imaging **38**(8), 1788–1800 (2019)
2. Familiari, A., et al.: Risk factors for coarctation of the aorta on prenatal ultrasound: a systematic review and meta-analysis. Circulation **135**(8), 772–785 (2017)
3. Grigorescu, I., et al.: Diffusion tensor driven image registration: a deep learning approach. In: Špiclin, Ž, McClelland, J., Kybic, J., Goksel, O. (eds.) WBIR 2020. LNCS, vol. 12120, pp. 131–140. Springer, Cham (2020). https://doi.org/10.1007/978-3-030-50120-4_13
4. Hermida, U., et al.: Learning the hidden signature of fetal arch anatomy: a three-dimensional shape analysis in suspected coarctation of the aorta. J. Cardiovasc. Transl. Res. **16**, 738–747 (2022)
5. Hermida, U., et al.: Simplifying disease staging models into a single anatomical axis-a case study of aortic coarctation in-utero. In: International Workshop on Statistical Atlases and Computational Models of the Heart, pp. 269–279. Springer, Heidelberg (2022). https://doi.org/10.1007/978-3-031-23443-9_25
6. Kainz, B., et al.: Fast volume reconstruction from motion corrupted stacks of 2d slices. IEEE Trans. Med. Imaging **34**(9), 1901–1913 (2015)
7. Kuklisova-Murgasova, M., Quaghebeur, G., Rutherford, M.A., Hajnal, J.V., Schnabel, J.A.: Reconstruction of fetal brain MRI with intensity matching and complete outlier removal. Med. Image Anal. **16**(8), 1550–1564 (2012)
8. Law, M.A., Tivakaran, V.S.: Coarctation of the aorta. In: StatPearls [Internet]. StatPearls Publishing (2022)
9. Lloyd, D.F., et al.: Three-dimensional visualisation of the fetal heart using prenatal MRI with motion-corrected slice-volume registration: a prospective, single-centre cohort study. Lancet **393**(10181), 1619–1627 (2019)
10. Lloyd, D.F., et al.: Analysis of 3-dimensional arch anatomy, vascular flow, and postnatal outcome in cases of suspected coarctation of the aorta using fetal cardiac magnetic resonance imaging. Circ. Cardiovasc. Imaging **14**(7), e012411 (2021)
11. Oktay, O., et al.: Attention u-net: learning where to look for the pancreas. arXiv preprint arXiv:1804.03999 (2018)
12. Ramirez Gilliland, P., et al.: Automated multi-class fetal cardiac vessel segmentation in aortic arch anomalies using t2-weighted 3D fetal MRI. In: International Workshop on Preterm, Perinatal and Paediatric Image Analysis, pp. 82–93. Springer, Heidelberg (2022). https://doi.org/10.1007/978-3-031-17117-8_8
13. Salehi, S.S.M., Erdogmus, D., Gholipour, A.: Tversky loss function for image segmentation using 3D fully convolutional deep networks. In: Wang, Q., Shi, Y., Suk, H.-I., Suzuki, K. (eds.) MLMI 2017. LNCS, vol. 10541, pp. 379–387. Springer, Cham (2017). https://doi.org/10.1007/978-3-319-67389-9_44

14. Uus, A., et al.: Deformable slice-to-volume registration for motion correction of fetal body and placenta MRI. IEEE Trans. Med. Imaging **39**(9), 2750–2759 (2020)
15. Uus, A.U., et al.: Automated 3D reconstruction of the fetal thorax in the standard atlas space from motion-corrupted MRI stacks for 21–36 weeks ga range. Med. Image Anal. **80**, 102484 (2022). https://doi.org/10.1016/j.media.2022.102484. https://www.sciencedirect.com/science/article/pii/S1361841522001311
16. Uus, A.U., et al.: 3D black blood cardiovascular magnetic resonance atlases of congenital aortic arch anomalies and the normal fetal heart: application to automated multi-label segmentation. J. Cardiovasc. Magn. Reson. **24**(1), 1–13 (2022)
17. Varela, M., et al.: Novel computational analysis of left atrial anatomy improves prediction of atrial fibrillation recurrence after ablation. Front. Physiol. **8**(FEB), 68 (2017). https://doi.org/10.3389/fphys.2017.00068
18. Xu, Z., Niethammer, M.: DeepAtlas: joint semi-supervised learning of image registration and segmentation. In: Shen, D., et al. (eds.) MICCAI 2019. LNCS, vol. 11765, pp. 420–429. Springer, Cham (2019). https://doi.org/10.1007/978-3-030-32245-8_47
19. Zhao, A., Balakrishnan, G., Durand, F., Guttag, J.V., Dalca, A.V.: Data augmentation using learned transformations for one-shot medical image segmentation. In: Proceedings of the IEEE/CVF Conference on Computer Vision and Pattern Recognition, pp. 8543–8553 (2019)

The Challenge of Fetal Cardiac MRI Reconstruction Using Deep Learning

Denis Prokopenko[1]([✉])(iD), Kerstin Hammernik[2,3], Thomas Roberts[1,4], David F. A. Lloyd[5,6], Daniel Rueckert[2,3], and Joseph V. Hajnal[1]

[1] Biomedical Engineering Department, School of Biomedical Engineering and Imaging Sciences, King's College London, London, UK
denis.prokopenko@kcl.ac.uk

[2] Department of Informatics, Technical University of Munich, Munich, Germany

[3] Department of Computing, Imperial College London, London, UK

[4] Clinical Scientific Computing, Guy's and St. Thomas' NHS Foundation Trust, London, UK

[5] Child Health, King's College London, London, UK

[6] Paediatric and Fetal Cardiology, Evelina London Children's Hospital, London, UK

Abstract. Dynamic free-breathing fetal cardiac MRI is one of the most challenging modalities, which requires high temporal and spatial resolution to depict rapid changes in a small fetal heart. The ability of deep learning methods to recover undersampled data could help to optimise the kt-SENSE acquisition strategy and improve non-gated kt-SENSE reconstruction quality. However, their application is limited by the lack of available fetal cardiac data. In this work, we explore supervised deep learning networks for reconstruction of kt-SENSE style acquired data using an extensive in vivo dataset. Having access to fully-sampled low-resolution multi-coil fetal cardiac MRI, we study the performance of the networks to recover fully-sampled data from undersampled data. We consider model architectures together with training strategies taking into account their application in the real clinical setup used to collect the dataset to enable networks to recover prospectively undersampled data. We explore a set of modifications to form a baseline performance evaluation for dynamic fetal cardiac MRI on real data. We systematically evaluate the models on coil-combined data to reveal the effect of the suggested changes to the architecture in the context of fetal heart properties. We show that the best-performing models recover a detailed depiction of the maternal anatomy on a large scale, but the dynamic properties of the fetal heart are under-represented. Training directly on multi-coil data improves the performance of the models, allows their prospective application to undersampled data and makes them outperform CTFNet introduced for adult cardiac cine MRI. However, these models deliver similar qualitative performances recovering the maternal body very well but underestimating the dynamic properties of fetal heart. This dynamic feature of fast change of fetal heart that is highly localised suggests both more targeted training and evaluation methods might be needed for fetal heart application.

Keywords: Image Reconstruction · Fetal Cardiac MRI · Deep Learning

D. Link-Sourani et al. (Eds.): PIPPI 2023, LNCS 14246, pp. 64–74, 2023.
https://doi.org/10.1007/978-3-031-45544-5_6

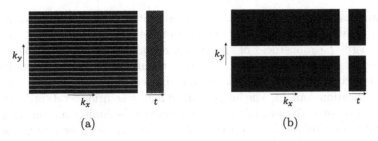

Fig. 1. The kt-SENSE acquisition patterns to sample high-resolution undersampled (a) and low-resolution densely sampled (b) kt data.

1   Introduction

Dynamic free-breathing fetal cardiac imaging is one of the most challenging applications of magnetic resonance imaging (MRI). Fetal heart imaging requires a large field of view to encompass the maternal anatomy combined with high spatial and temporal resolutions to depict tiny dynamic structures of the fetal heart. The imaging must accommodate uncontrolled fetal motion and maternal respiration while capturing fetal cardiac beating, which could be more than twice as fast as an adult heartbeat.

Conventional kt-SENSE [22] can deliver dynamic MRI of fetal heart across multiple cardiac cycles using a prior-led reconstruction of highly undersampled signals. While there are other reconstruction methods to deliver dynamic fetal cardiac MRI using non-Cartesian or non-uniform sampling [6, 12] or gating [5, 11], we focus on the kt-SENSE approach as it was used to acquire the substantial dataset of fetal cardiac MRI. The kt-SENSE is simpler to use to collect the data compared to non-uniform or non-Cartesian methods and provides real-time fetal cardiac data over multiple cardiac cycles without averaging in contrast to gated approaches. In case of kt-SENSE, the data is usually acquired in two stages using sampling patterns, which have high temporal resolution to freeze bulk fetal and fetal cardiac motion. One acquisition pattern in Fig. 1a samples high-resolution undersampled k-space data in time (kt data). The other pattern in Fig. 1b acquires low-resolution (low k) fully-sampled kt data, which helps to disambiguate dynamic features in undersampled data during reconstruction. However, the two-stage acquisition approach is inefficient because the same anatomy is sampled twice, while changes in fetal pose between the two samplings could introduce differences in the collected data reducing the quality of the reconstruction.

Recent advances in deep learning (DL) for dynamic adult cardiac MRI reconstruction [3, 16–18, 21] expanded the variety of methods that can be used for the reconstruction. The ability to recover fully-sampled data directly from under-sampled information is a common aim of the proposed DL reconstruction methods. In the case of fetal cardiac MRI, they have the potential to replace the dense acquisition part (Fig. 1b) with a reconstruction from data acquired with undersampling pattern (Fig. 1a). As a result, it could reduce the acquisition time up to two times, using only one part of the two-stage sampling approach, and increase the robustness of the reconstruction to the spontaneous motion between the stages of acquisition. However, the use of DL reconstruction methods for fetal cardiac MRI reconstruction is limited due to additional constraints of the application domain. The fully-sampled high-resolution fetal cardiac ground truth data is currently unavailable. This is due to the limitations on the spatio-temporal resolution required to freeze the motion and scanner acquisition rate. Also, the lack of real high-resolution dynamic MRI data forces DL methods to employ high-resolution reconstructions as ground truth. As a result, the models are optimised to mimic the target reconstruction algorithms with their biases rather than the true depiction of the anatomy. In addition, the networks usually perform dynamic adult heart MRI reconstruction from retrospectively under-sampled gated cine modality, which differs from the fetal cardiac case, where the recovery of the heartbeat over multiple cycles is desired. In the absence of the ground truth data, emerged self-supervised versions showed similar performance to supervised models according to the numerical evaluations [1, 24]. However, the self-supervised models delivered a less reliable depiction of the moving edges, which are the most sensitive anatomy in the case of fetal cardiac MRI.

In this work, we study the performance of supervised DL baselines to recover fully-sampled low-resolution dynamic fetal cardiac MRI from undersampled data to make the kt-SENSE [22] algorithm more robust to motion and shorten the acquisition time. First, we present and compare a set of U-Net-based architectures trained on data combined over multiple coils (coil-combined) to recover undersampled data, focusing on dynamic properties of fetal heart. Next, we take the best-performing versions and present their performance being trained on multi-coil data, which enables their prospective application to the existing kt-SENSE acquisition and reconstruction pipelines and direct comparison with the state-of-the-art Complementary Time-Frequency domain Network (CTFNet) proposed for gated adult heart MRI reconstruction.

2   Methods

We investigate the reconstruction of free-breathing dynamic fetal heart MRI volumes acquired with a multi-coil receiver array as a part of kt-SENSE [22] algorithm. We use the fully-sampled low-resolution data acquired from scanner to study DL methods to recover real depiction of anatomy rather than mimicking conventional reconstruction algorithms with their biases. The data is sampled in kt space, but it can be represented in temporal image space (xt) and temporal frequency image space (xf) as well. First, we use the coil-combined SENSE [15] data to study the reconstruction quality of dynamic features of fetal heart using a set of modified U-Net models [20]. Next, we take the best-performing models and train them directly on multi-coil data to use the advantages of the diverse coil data. Training on coil data allows us to optimise the models in a clinically relevant way to work with the undersampled data acquired prospectively from

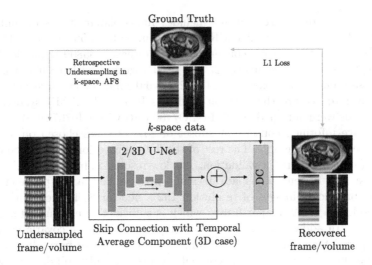

Fig. 2. The architecture with optional data consistency (DC) layer [21] and skip connection propagating temporal average. The skip connection is used for 3D models trained on data in the xf domain.

the scanner. Finally, we compare the models with an iterative Complementary Time-Frequency Domain Network (CTFNet) [16], which was introduced as a state-of-the-art method for adult cine MRI reconstruction.

The 2D version of the U-Net based model with optional data consistency (DC) layer [21] in Fig. 2 processes each complex-valued image frame in xt space independently without explicitly exploiting the spatio-temporal correlations available in fetal cardiac data. To enrich the input with temporal information, we add a sliding window average or a temporal average to the undersampled data as additional input channels. The sliding window average is a sum of R consecutive image frames, where $R = 8$ is the acceleration factor of undersampling. Temporal averaging delivers an average of all frames scaled by acceleration factor R.

The 3D version of the U-Net based model with an optional DC layer [21] in Fig. 2 processes the volumes that contain all available temporal information within the slice volume. In contrast to the 2D case, the 3D models can process data in the temporal frequency (xf) domain, which is a sparser representation than the xt representation and usually helps to improve the reconstruction quality [13,22]. Since the xf representation has most of the energy concentrated in the temporal average frame, the optimisation of the loss function is likely to favour reconstruction of the temporal average rather than the lower energy dynamic temporal frequencies. To shift the focus to non-zero frequency frames, we add the temporal average to the 3D U-Net output via a skip connection shown in Fig. 2.

Our fetal cardiac MRI dataset includes multi-planar stacks of multi-slice multi-coil dynamic fetal cardiac MRI scans acquired from 56 subjects (3 healthy volunteers, 53 patients with congenital heart diseases, 55809 dynamic 3D coil volumes). The bSSFP sequence [2] was used together with regular Cartesian kt undersampling [23], voxel size $2.0 \times 2.0 \times 6.0$ mm, $8\times$ acceleration, and 28 coil receiver to acquire the data on a Philips Ingenia 1.5T MR system. Ethical approvals were obtained (REC 14/LO/1806, REC 07/H0707/105), and each subject gave informed consent. A subset of 20% of cases chosen on a patient level is used for testing only. The rest of the data is used for training the models with 20% of it set apart for validation. The low-resolution fully-sampled signal is sampled across 19 central k-space lines and zero-padded in the phase-encoding direction producing images of resolution 152×400 for 64 frames, with a temporal resolution of 72 ms per frame, which is sufficient to capture fetal cardiac motion [19]. In addition, coil sensitivity maps and coil noise covariance matrix were acquired for each multi-coil volume, which we use to normalise the data to the unit noise level. While the coil data forms our multi-coil dataset, we create an additional coil-combined dataset by combining coil data using SENSE reconstruction [15]. To mimic the kt-SENSE [22] acquisition sampling used to collect the dataset, we retrospectively undersample data with the uniform lattice pattern [23] and acceleration factor $R = 8$.

The U-Net architectures follow the original implementation [20] with convolutional kernel size 3 and 4 downsampling steps with 2×2 max pooling. The optional data consistency (DC) layer has three modes: no DC, forced DC and adjustable DC. The forced option replaces the output of the model with available input data, while the adjustable option uses a merging coefficient which is optimised as an additional model parameter. For both datasets, the U-Net modifications were trained to optimise the $\mathcal{L}_1$ loss function for 50 epochs using Adam [9] with a learning rate of 0.0001 and exponential decay of 0.95 using the PyTorch framework [14]. The final set of model parameters is chosen based on the performance of the models on the validation subset.

In the case of CTFNet, the architecture follows the original implementation and training procedure [16]. The model was tuned over 150 epochs optimising the $\mathcal{L}_1$ loss function on the patches using Adam with the same learning rate and decay as for U-Net-based architectures. In addition, we used adjustable DC coefficient to merge the available input information into model prediction.

The evaluation is performed for 14 modifications of U-Net trained on the coil-combined dataset and for the 3 best-performing versions of U-Net together with CTFNet trained on multi-coil data. The quantitative evaluation compares coil-combined predicted volumes and ground truth data in the xt domain per volume according to normalised mean squared error (NMSE), mean squared error (MSE), mean absolute error (MAE), peak signal-to-noise ratio (PSNR) and structural similarity (SSIM) over a masked body region. While the NMSE, MSE and MAE compare tensors with complex intensities, magnitude tensors are evaluated using PyTorch Image Quality (PIQ) [8] implementation of PSNR and

Table 1. Comparison of the U-Net models trained on coil-combined dataset.

Model description	NMSE ↓	MSE ↓	MAE ↓	PSNR ↑	SSIM ↑
2D U-Net, no DC	0.7976	4102.3838	49.3082	12.2359	0.6209
2D U-Net, adjustable (adj.) DC	0.7829	4019.8306	49.0102	12.3327	0.6324
2D U-Net, forced DC	0.7715	3967.0254	49.1194	12.3991	0.6393
2D U-Net, sliding window	0.0062	32.0378	4.1111	33.7646	0.9826
2D U-Net, temporal average	0.0176	91.4503	5.7255	29.6221	0.9658
3D U-Net, xt, no DC	0.0130	67.1712	5.7132	30.2262	0.9678
3D U-Net, xt, adj. DC	0.0108	55.7603	5.3444	31.0387	0.9710
3D U-Net, xt, forced DC	0.0107	55.1941	5.3293	31.0834	0.9713
3D U-Net, xf, no DC	0.0097	50.7774	4.8127	31.6965	0.9742
3D U-Net, xf, adj. DC	0.0091	47.1734	4.7795	32.0303	0.9772
3D U-Net, xf, forced DC	0.0087	45.5490	4.7054	32.2168	0.9774
3D U-Net, xf, skip connect, no DC	0.0053	27.7157	3.6231	34.4853	0.9854
3D U-Net, xf, skip connect, adj. DC	**0.0049**	25.5143	3.5402	34.8319	0.9863
3D U-Net, xf, skip connect, forced DC	**0.0049**	**25.3647**	**3.5373**	**34.8663**	**0.9864**

SSIM [7]. The presence of important dynamic features of fetal heart is evaluated visually in temporal and frequency domains.

3   Results

In case of model optimisation using coil-combined data, the best results were shown by 3D U-Nets with temporal average skip connection and data consistency trained using the xf representation of data. The model managed to deliver the best values according to evaluated metrics for both forced and adjustable modes of data consistency layer (Table 1). The next best performance was achieved using the same model without data consistency. Qualitatively, the models were highly effective at recovering accurate image depictions of static or slowly moving maternal and fetal anatomy as revealed by the subtraction images in Fig. 3. Even though the 3D U-Net with data consistency and skip connection delivered the closest to ground truth results for rapid changes in small regions such as fetal heart, there was still a clear under-representation of the beating of a tiny heart seen in both temporal and frequency domains.

Additional access to temporal information played a crucial role in improving the performance of the trained models. In the simplest case of a 2D U-Net with DC, the frame-wise training approach fails to deliver reliable results with model overfitting on training data. Temporal average and sliding window average information supplied with the input boosted the performance for all evaluated metrics compared to 2D U-Net without access to an additional input of temporal information. The additional inputs helped to improve the 2D U-Net performance reducing the NMSE more than 100 and almost 50 times for sliding window and temporal average injections respectively and improving the SSIM to 0.9826 and

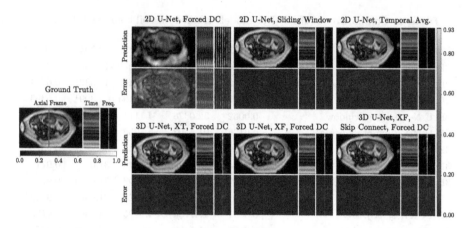

Fig. 3. Comparison of the models trained on coil-combined dataset. The figure shows axial frame view and a slice through fetal heart (red line) in temporal (xt) and frequency (xf) domains for ground truth volume and each model prediction with the corresponding error maps. (Color figure online)

Table 2. Comparison of the models trained on multi-coil dataset.

Model description	NMSE ↓	MSE ↓	MAE ↓	PSNR ↑	SSIM ↑
CTFNet, adj. DC	0.0082	52.2186	3.5009	34.6011	0.9869
3D U-Net, xf, skip connect, no DC	**0.0032**	16.5106	2.7226	36.9108	0.9897
3D U-Net, xf, skip connect, adj. DC	**0.0032**	16.3916	2.7202	36.9298	0.9897
3D U-Net, xf, skip connect, forced DC	**0.0032**	**16.3363**	**2.7088**	**36.9645**	**0.9898**

0.9658. The same trend can be seen in Fig. 3 as the models are able to recover the main features of a slice, while 2D U-Net with sliding window resolved some slow dynamic features as well.

All variants of 3D U-Net showed improved performance compared to the 2D U-Net with DC according to evaluated metrics. Qualitatively, 3D models recovered more information about anatomy movements and resolved aliasing artefacts slightly better. The 3D U-Net case showed positive changes in model performance moving from a temporal representation of the data to a sparser xf domain and additional propagation of temporal average via skip connection. The combination of sparse data representation and skip connection helped to outperform 2D U-Net with sliding window, recovering a more detailed depiction of the fetal heart beating in both temporal and frequency domains (Fig. 3).

The introduction of a data consistency layer enhanced the performance of all U-Net-based models and improved the evaluated metrics (Table 1). The forced mode for DC enabled slightly better performance across the models than an adjustable injection of the available input into output.

In the case of multi-coil data, three versions of 3D U-Net in xf domain with skip connection and CTFNet were fine-tuned and compared. The 3D U-Net

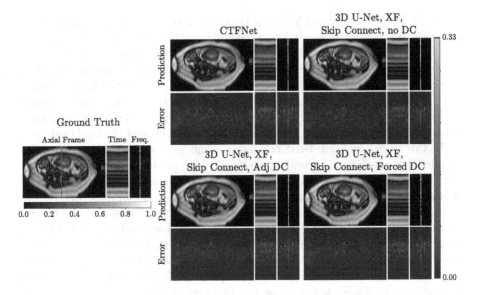

Fig. 4. Comparison of the models trained on multi-coil dataset. The figure shows axial frame view and a slice through fetal heart (red line) in temporal (xt) and frequency (xf) domains for ground truth volume and each model prediction with the corresponding error maps. (Color figure online)

with skip connection in xf space and forced DC delivered the best performance (Table 2). The 3D U-Net with adjustable and no DC showed the second and the third-best results, outperforming the state-of-the-art CTFNet model proposed for a superficially similar task of adult heart reconstruction. The image representation of prediction delivered by the best-performing 3D U-Net has similar to the ground truth depiction of the anatomy in Fig. 4. However, the dynamic features of the recovered fetal heart remain underrepresented in both temporal and frequency domains.

4   Discussion

In this work, we studied the reconstruction quality of kt-SENSE acquired fetal heart MRIs introducing gradual improvements to the U-Net backbone model. Most of the modifications delivered faithful reconstructions of the maternal anatomy and some dynamic features of adult breathing and fetal motion. The best performance was delivered by the 3D U-Net with forced DC and skip connection optimised on xf data representations. The quantitative evaluation reported excellent performance according to estimated global image measures. The reconstruction results showed a clear depiction of the maternal and main fetal features. However, there is a room for further improvements to recover the highly-dynamic features of fetal heart.

The CTFNet performed less well than the best U-Net architectures by all measures. It was able to recover the large-scale anatomy, but the periodic dynamics and tiny fetal heart size limited the reconstruction of fetal heartbeat.

Notable performance was shown by the 2D U-Net with sliding window, which outperformed the basic 3D U-Net, even though the latter should have benefited from access to all available frames. It is evident that the sliding window average is highly effective at resolving the aliasing artefacts preserving slower time variations. Still, the reconstructed details could not fully represent the fetal heartbeat.

In this work, we considered training the models to recover real-time fully-sampled low-resolution ground truth from data undersampled with uniform Cartesian undersampling pattern and acceleration factor 8. Such data strategy allows us to incorporate the presented models trained on coil data directly into existing fetal cardiac MRI pipelines based on kt-SENSE acquisition used to sample the dataset. In addition, the use of fully-sampled low-resolution data helps to avoid biases that models could grasp from learning high-resolution reconstruction delivered by conventional methods. While one could use other acquisition planning with non-uniform non-Cartesian patterns, lower acceleration factor or data binning to deliver better reconstruction quality [4, 10, 16, 18], the produced results would be out of touch with the acquisition procedure used to collect the dataset used in our study.

The presented results showed that the metrics helped to evaluate the global reconstruction quality. However, they were less effective in describing the errors that only occur in small spatial regions. Therefore, we believe that more localised metrics together with more advanced backbone architectures could push further the reconstruction quality of fetal heart delivered by the DL models. While the local measures could help to address the unbalanced dynamic features in data, a more complex backbone could include explicit features focused on motion reconstruction.

5   Conclusion

In this work, we studied the challenge of fetal cardiac MRI reconstruction using deep learning models. We progressively improved the performance of the U-Net backbone by introducing a set of modifications, which resulted in a systematic comparison of 14 versions of the model and the cutting-edge CTFNet, designed for adult cardiac imaging. The most effective model was 3D U-Net with data consistency and temporal average skip connection trained in xf domain according to both qualitative and quantitative assessments. The CTFNet model designed for adult imaging data was not that effective for fetal cardiac reconstruction, highlighting the more challenging nature of the fetal heart compared to the adult heart. The best-performing networks were highly effective at recovering the large-scale field of view. However, they were unable to fully recover the detailed dynamic features of the fetal heart. This feature of fast change that is highly localised suggests both more targeted training and evaluation methods might be needed for fetal heart application. Exploring these will be the subject of future work.

Acknowledgements. We appreciate the funding from EPSRC Centre for Doctoral Training in Smart Medical Imaging EP/S022104/1, support from Philips Medical Systems and core funding from the Wellcome/EPSRC Centre for Medical Engineering WT 203148/Z/16/Z and NIHR Biomedical Research Centre at Guy's and St Thomas' NHS Trust.

References

1. Acar, M., Çukur, T., Öksüz, İ.: Self-supervised dynamic MRI reconstruction. In: Machine Learning for Medical Image Reconstruction: 4th International Workshop, MLMIR 2021, Held in Conjunction with MICCAI 2021, Strasbourg, France, 1 October 2021, Proceedings 4, pp. 35–44. Springer, Cham (2021). https://doi.org/10.1007/978-3-030-88552-6_4

2. Carr, H.: Steady-state free precession in nuclear magnetic resonance. Phys. Rev. **112**(5), 1693 (1958)

3. Desai, A.D., et al.: Noise2Recon: a semi-supervised framework for joint MRI reconstruction and denoising. arXiv preprint arXiv:2110.00075 (2021)

4. Hammernik, K., et al.: Learning a variational network for reconstruction of accelerated MRI data. Magn. Reson. Med. **79**(6), 3055–3071 (2018)

5. Haris, K., et al.: Self-gated fetal cardiac MRI with tiny golden angle iGRASP: a feasibility study. J. Magn. Reson. Imaging **46**(1), 207–217 (2017)

6. Jung, H., Sung, K., Nayak, K.S., Kim, E.Y., Ye, J.C.: k-t FOCUSS a general compressed sensing framework for high resolution dynamic MRI. Magn. Reson. Med. Official J. Int. Soc. Magn. Reson. Med. **61**(1), 103–116 (2009)

7. Kastryulin, S., Zakirov, D., Prokopenko, D.: PyTorch Image Quality: Metrics and measure for image quality assessment (2019). Open-source software available at https://github.com/photosynthesis-team/piq

8. Kastryulin, S., Zakirov, J., Prokopenko, D., Dylov, D.V.: PyTorch image quality: metrics for image quality assessment. arXiv preprint arXiv:2208.14818 (2022)

9. Kingma, D.P., Ba, J.: Adam: a method for stochastic optimization. arXiv preprint arXiv:1412.6980 (2014)

10. Kofler, A., Dewey, M., Schaeffter, T., Wald, C., Kolbitsch, C.: Spatio-temporal deep learning-based undersampling artefact reduction for 2D radial cine MRI with limited training data. IEEE Trans. Med. Imaging **39**(3), 703–717 (2019)

11. Kording, F., et al.: Dynamic fetal cardiovascular magnetic resonance imaging using doppler ultrasound gating. J. Cardiovasc. Magn. Reson. **20**(1), 1–10 (2018)

12. Lingala, S.G., Hu, Y., DiBella, E., Jacob, M.: Accelerated dynamic MRI exploiting sparsity and low-rank structure: k-t SLR. IEEE Trans. Med. Imaging **30**(5), 1042–1054 (2011)

13. Lustig, M., Donoho, D., Pauly, J.M.: Sparse MRI: the application of compressed sensing for rapid MR imaging. Magn. Reson. Med. Official J. Int. Soc. Magn. Reson. Med. **58**(6), 1182–1195 (2007)

14. Paszke, A., et al.: PyTorch: an imperative style, high-performance deep learning library. In: Advances in Neural Information Processing Systems, vol. 32 (2019)

15. Pruessmann, K.P., Weiger, M., Scheidegger, M.B., Boesiger, P.: Sense: sensitivity encoding for fast MRI. Magn. Reson. Med. Official J. Int. Soc. Magn. Reson. Med. **42**(5), 952–962 (1999)

16. Qin, C., et al.: Complementary time-frequency domain networks for dynamic parallel MR image reconstruction. Magn. Reson. Med. **86**(6), 3274–3291 (2021)

17. Qin, C., Schlemper, J., Caballero, J., Price, A.N., Hajnal, J.V., Rueckert, D.: Convolutional recurrent neural networks for dynamic MR image reconstruction. IEEE Trans. Med. Imaging **38**(1), 280–290 (2018)

18. Qin, C., et al.: k-t NEXT: dynamic MR image reconstruction exploiting spatiotemporal correlations. In: Shen, D., et al. (eds.) MICCAI 2019. LNCS, vol. 11765, pp. 505–513. Springer, Cham (2019). https://doi.org/10.1007/978-3-030-32245-8_56

19. Roberts, T.A., et al.: Fetal whole heart blood flow imaging using 4D cine MRI. Nat. Commun. **11**(1), 1–13 (2020)

20. Ronneberger, O., Fischer, P., Brox, T.: U-Net: convolutional networks for biomedical image segmentation. In: Navab, N., Hornegger, J., Wells, W.M., Frangi, A.F. (eds.) MICCAI 2015. LNCS, vol. 9351, pp. 234–241. Springer, Cham (2015). https://doi.org/10.1007/978-3-319-24574-4_28

21. Schlemper, J., Caballero, J., Hajnal, J.V., Price, A., Rueckert, D.: A deep cascade of convolutional neural networks for dynamic MR image reconstruction. In: International Conference on Information Processing in Medical Imaging, pp. 647–658. Springer, Cham (2017)

22. Tsao, J., Boesiger, P., Pruessmann, K.P.: k-t BLAST and k-t SENSE: dynamic MRI with high frame rate exploiting spatiotemporal correlations. Magn. Reson. Med. Official J. Int. Soc. Magn. Reson. Med. **50**(5), 1031–1042 (2003)

23. Tsao, J., Kozerke, S., Boesiger, P., Pruessmann, K.P.: Optimizing spatiotemporal sampling for k-t BLAST and k-t SENSE: application to high-resolution real-time cardiac steady-state free precession. Magn. Reson. Med. Official J. Int. Soc. Magn. Reson. Med. **53**(6), 1372–1382 (2005)

24. Zou, J., et al.: SelfCoLearn: self-supervised collaborative learning for accelerating dynamic MR imaging. Bioengineering **9**(11), 650 (2022)

Placental and Cervical Image Analysis

Consistency Regularization Improves Placenta Segmentation in Fetal EPI MRI Time Series

Yingcheng Liu[1(✉)], Neerav Karani[1], S. Mazdak Abulnaga[1], Junshen Xu[2], P. Ellen Grant[3], Esra Abaci Turk[3], and Polina Golland[1]

[1] Computer Science and Artificial Intelligence Lab, Massachusetts Institute of Technology, Cambridge 02139, USA
{liuyc,nkarani,abulnaga,junshen}@mit.edu, polina@csail.mit.edu
[2] Department of Electrical Engineering and Computer Science, Massachusetts Institute of Technology, Cambridge, MA 02139, USA
[3] Fetal-Neonatal Neuroimaging and Developmental Science Center, Boston Children's Hospital, Harvard Medical School, Boston, MA 02115, USA
{ellen.grant,esra.abaciturk}@childrens.harvard.edu

Abstract. The placenta plays a crucial role in fetal development. Automated 3D placenta segmentation from fetal EPI MRI holds promise for advancing prenatal care. This paper proposes an effective semi-supervised learning method for improving placenta segmentation in fetal EPI MRI time series. We introduce consistency regularization loss that promotes consistency under spatial transformation of the same image and temporal consistency across nearby images in a time series. The experimental results show that the method improves the overall segmentation accuracy and provides better performance for outliers and hard samples. The evaluation also indicates that our method improves the temporal coherency of the prediction, which could lead to more accurate computation of temporal placental biomarkers. This work contributes to the study of the placenta and prenatal clinical decision-making.

Keywords: Fetal MRI · image segmentation · semi-supervised learning (SSL) · consistency regularization · placenta segmentation

1 Introduction

In this paper, we propose an effective semi-supervised learning method that improves the segmentation of the placenta in fetal EPI MRI time series. The automatic 3D segmentation of the placenta facilitates better population studies [11], visualization of individual placentae for monitoring and assessment [1], and intervention planning.

The promise of automated placenta segmentation in 3D MRI has been previously demonstrated [2,3,15]. Neural networks provide state-of-the-art performance and have emerged as the most popular paradigm [2,3]. However, one shortcoming of deep learning methods is that they require a large number of annotated training examples. Manual segmentation of placenta is difficult in

© The Author(s), under exclusive license to Springer Nature Switzerland AG 2023
D. Link-Sourani et al. (Eds.): PIPPI 2023, LNCS 14246, pp. 77–87, 2023.
https://doi.org/10.1007/978-3-031-45544-5_7

temporal 3D MRI imaging due to inherently 3D shape of the placenta and due to deformations caused by maternal breathing, contractions, and fetal motion. Furthermore, functional EPI images of the placenta have lower in-plane resolution than anatomical HASTE volumes. The contrast between the organ and the surrounding anatomy is worse, making it challenging to determine the placental boundary. These issues preclude annotation of large datasets, thereby hindering the development of accurate neural network models.

One possible solution to this problem is semi-supervised learning, which promises to yield performant neural network models while requiring only a partial labeling of the dataset. One line of work promotes consistency between labeled and unlabeled data. For example, encouraging consistency of the feature embedding distribution between labeled and unlabeled data regularizes the model's training either directly [4] or via adversarial learning [9]. Another line of work uses unlabeled and labeled data sequentially in different training stages by first pre-training an image representation on a large unlabeled dataset and then fine-tuning the segmentation model with a small labeled dataset [16,17].

In this paper, we build on the third strategy of integrating semi-supervised learning into the training of a placental segmentation network. Our method is based on consistency regularization, a class of semi-supervised learning methods that promotes the invariance and equivariance of model predictions. The idea is to make the segmentation predictions consistent between two different augmented versions of the same image. We refer to this consistency as spatial consistency. Applying existing spatial consistency regularization methods [8,12,19] to our data only emphasizes the consistency within the same image but ignores the relationships among different images in a time series. To encourage temporal consistency, we leverage the fact that our dataset is a collection of time series. Given the minor deformation of placenta between consecutive frames, temporal consistency regularization encourages the model predictions on two consecutive frames to be similar. If the registration of the placental region were available, one could require exact temporal consistency similar to its spatial counterpart. Alternatively, one could use robust measures of consistency and only penalize very large misalignments. In this preliminary study, we evaluate the promise of the idea by implementing a simple consistency loss term. We leave in-depth analysis of more principled alternatives to future work.

To implement spatial and temporal consistency, we employ a two-branch Siamese architecture during training [7]. Each branch in the Siamese network receives a different image as input (either spatially transformed versions of the same image or close frames in the time series) and is supervised to output predictions consistent with the other branch.

We evaluate our method on a dataset of 3D EPI MRI placenta time series of 91 subjects. We show that our method provides modest but robust improvements on average, and significantly improves the quality of segmentation in the outlier cases. The results also suggest that our method is more efficient than other semi-supervised learning methods such as mean teacher [18] and self-training [21].

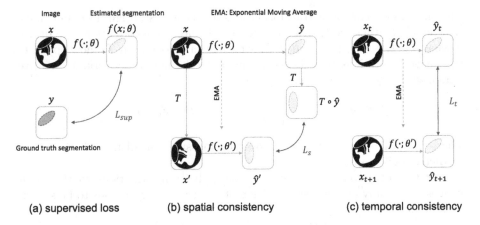

(a) supervised loss   (b) spatial consistency   (c) temporal consistency

Fig. 1. Overview of Consistency Regularization Training Scheme. Our consistency regularization loss includes three parts: (a) supervised segmentation loss (b) spatial consistency regularization loss that promotes consistency within the same sample (c) temporal consistency regularization loss that encourages the predictions to be similar between consecutive frames in the time series. When using the teacher-student training for (b) and (c), we use the exponential moving average (EMA) of the student model to update the teacher model.

2   Methods

In this section, we will first define spatial and temporal consistency regularization loss central to our method in Sect. 2.1, describe the Siamese training architecture and its teacher-student variant in Sect. 2.2. Last, we provide implementation details in Sect. 2.3. The high-level overview of our training scheme is illustrated in Fig. 1.

2.1   Consistency Regularization Loss

Let $\mathcal{X}_l = \{(x_i, y_i), i = 1, 2, ..., n\}$ and $\mathcal{X}_u = \{x_i, i = 1, 2, ..., m\}$ be the labeled and unlabeled data, where $x_i \in \mathbb{R}^{H \times W \times D}$ is a 3D MRI image and $y_i \in \{0, 1, 2, ..., C-1\}^{H \times W \times D}$ is the ground truth segmentation label map with C distinct classes ($C = 2$ in our application). A neural network segmentation model predicts a segmentation map $\hat{y} = \sigma(f(x; \theta)) \in \mathbb{R}^{H \times W \times D}$ from an input image x, where $\sigma(\cdot)$ is a softmax function and $f(x; \theta)$ is the logits map of the neural network parameterized by θ. Ground truth label maps are used to minimize supervised loss $\mathcal{L}_{\text{sup}}(\theta) = \mathbb{E}_{(x,y) \in \mathcal{X}_l} \mathcal{S}(f(x; \theta), y)$ for image segmentation loss function $\mathcal{S}(\cdot, \cdot)$

The central idea of consistency regularization is to explicitly encourage the segmentation model to be invariant or equivariant to a certain group of transformations. We apply this idea both to the same input image and across different images in the time series. First, we regularize the segmentation models to be equivariant to geometric transformations (e.g., rigid or elastic transformations) while invariant to intensity transformations (e.g., contrast, brightness, and Gaussian noise). During the training of the model, these transformations are drawn stochastically from a pre-defined transformation distribution $\mathcal{T}$ and applied to the image before it is provided as an input to the neural network. We aim to minimize the spatial consistency loss term

$$\mathcal{L}_s(\theta) = \mathop{\mathbb{E}}_{T \sim \mathcal{T}, x \in \mathcal{X}_l \cup \mathcal{X}_u} \ell\Big(T \circ f(x;\theta), f(T \circ x;\theta)\Big), \tag{1}$$

where ℓ is a pixel-level consistency loss that measures the distance between two predicted logit maps.

For temporal consistency, we do not apply transformations to the input images but simply ask the segmentation of consecutive predictions to be similar by minimizing

$$\mathcal{L}_t(\theta) = \mathop{\mathbb{E}}_{x \in \mathcal{X}_u} \ell\Big(f(x;\theta), f(x';\theta)\Big), \tag{2}$$

where $\langle x, x' \rangle$ pair is constructed from two consecutive frames in the same MRI time series. Since consistency losses do not rely on ground truth segmentation labels, all unlabeled data can be incorporated into the training process.

Combining, we optimize parameters θ to minimize

$$\begin{aligned}
\mathcal{L}(\theta) &= \mathcal{L}_{\text{sup}}(\theta) + \lambda_1 \mathcal{L}_s(\theta; \mathcal{T}) + \lambda_2 \mathcal{L}_t(\theta) \\
&= \mathop{\mathbb{E}}_{(x,y) \in \mathcal{X}_l} \mathcal{S}(f(x;\theta), y) + \lambda_1 \mathop{\mathbb{E}}_{T \sim \mathcal{T}, x \in \mathcal{X}_l \cup \mathcal{X}_u} \ell\Big(T \circ f(x;\theta), f(T \circ x;\theta)\Big) \\
&\quad + \lambda_2 \mathop{\mathbb{E}}_{x \in \mathcal{X}_u} \ell\Big(f(x;\theta), f(x';\theta)\Big),
\end{aligned} \tag{3}$$

where λ_1, λ_2 are regularization parameters.

2.2   Siamese Neural Network

We use the U-Net architecture [14] as our segmentation model. We employ the so-called Siamese architecture to minimize the consistency loss terms. Specifically, one copy of the network operates on the current input image x, while another copy takes augmented image $T \circ x$ for spatial consistency and next frame x' for temporal consistency. Differences between the two segmentations are used to update the network weights. This training scheme has been widely applied to several problems such as object tracking [5] and representation learning [6].

Teacher-student variant of this Siamese design is known to be beneficial in many semi-supervised learning problems [8,12]. More specifically, the "teacher" branch of the model is decoupled from the gradient descent update process, and its weights are updated using the exponential moving average of the "student" model. Specifically, the weight of teacher model θ'_k is updated using $\theta'_k = \alpha \theta'_{k-1} + (1 - \alpha)\theta_k$, where θ_k is the student model parameters in iteration k of training, and α is a smoothing coefficient. Prior evidence shows that the teacher model has more stable predictions than the student model and provides more accurate supervision [8,12]. Another practical consideration of this architecture is that the teacher-student network is more computationally efficient. Since the teacher model is updated through exponential moving average, it takes up minimum GPU memory in the training process and saves approximately half of the memory compared to vanilla methods.

2.3   Implementation Details

In practice, we approximate the minimization of the objective above using batch stochastic gradient descent. At each step of the gradient descent, we sample a set of data $\mathcal{D} = \mathcal{D}_l \cup \mathcal{D}_{u_i}$, where $\mathcal{D}_l$ is uniformly sampled from labeled data $\mathcal{X}_l$ and $\mathcal{D}_{u_i}$ is uniformly sampled from unlabeled data $\mathcal{X}_u$. We make these datasets to have the same size (i.e. $|\mathcal{D}_l| = |\mathcal{D}_{u_i}|$). For each sample $x \in \mathcal{D}$, we independently draw a transformation T_i from $\mathcal{T}$ and retrieve the next frame $x' \in \mathcal{D}_u$.

To construct image transformation T, we sequentially apply the following transformations: random flipping along all dimensions with $p = 0.5$, random rotation along all dimensions with $p = 0.5$, random translation along all dimensions with $p = 0.1$ where displacements for each dimension are sampled from $\mathcal{U}(0, 5)$, random gamma transform with γ sampled from a uniform distribution $\mathcal{U}(0.5, 2)$, and random pixel-wise Gaussian noise with zero mean and σ sampled from a uniform distribution $\mathcal{U}(0, 0.1)$. We encourage the logit maps to be equivariant under random flipping, rotation, and translation transform while invariant to the random gamma and Gaussian noise transforms. Specifically, the transformation of the logitd map contains only the random flipping, rotation, and translation transform of the corresponding image transformation.

We modify λ_1 and λ_2 during the training following prior practice [8,12]. Specifically, we use $\lambda_i = \lambda_0 \exp\left(-5(1 - \frac{S}{L})^2\right)$ when $S \leq L$, where S is the current training step and L is the ramp-up length, $i = 1, 2$. When $S > L$, λ_i is set to λ_0. We set L to be half of the total training steps. The intuition behind this schedule is that the regularization is only necessary at the later stage of the training where overfitting is more severe. We use three lambda values ($\lambda_i = 0.01, 0.001, 0.0001$) for λ_1 and λ_2. And we report results for the best-performing model on the validation set.

We used DiceCE loss (i.e., sum of Dice loss and cross entropy loss) as our supervised segmentation loss and pixel-wise L2 distance between logits as our consistency loss. We use the Adam optimizer [10] with a learning rate of 10^{-4} and weight decay of 10^{-5}. We trained the model for 5000 epochs with batch size 16. We used linear warmup for 10 epochs and then a cosine annealing learning rate scheduler. All experiments are performed on a workstation with four NVIDIA 2080Ti GPUs. Each experiment takes about six hours to finish.

3   Experiments

In this section, we evaluate the proposed consistency regularization method on a set of research fetal EPI MRI time series.

3.1   Dataset

Our dataset consists of EPI MRI scans of 91 subjects, of which 78 were singleton pregnancies (gestational age (GA) of 23wk5d–37wk6d), and 13 were monochorionic-diamniotic (Mo-Di) twins (GA at MRI scan of 27wk5d–34wk5d). The cohort includes 63 healthy, 16 fetal growth restriction (FGR), and 12 high BMI (BMI > 30) pregnancies.

MRI scans were acquired on a 3T Siemens Skyra scanner (GRE-EPI, interleaved with 3mm isotropic voxels, TR $= 5.8$–8 s, TE $= 32 - 47$ ms, FA $= 90°$). We split the acquired interleaved volumes into two separate volumes with spacing $3 \times 3 \times 6$ mm, then linearly interpolated to $3 \times 3 \times 3$ mm.

The median of the length of the time series was 216 frames with interquartile range (IQR) of 125. The placenta was manually segmented by a trained rater. For each MRI time series, between 1 to 6 EPI volumes were manual segmentated, yielding a total of 176 ground truth labelmaps.

3.2   Baseline Methods

To understand the effect of different components of the consistency, we train the model with four different settings: basic model trained on labeled data using only the supervised loss L_{sup} (*Basic*), model trained using segmentation loss with spatial transformation consistency regularization $L_{\mathrm{sup}} + \lambda L_{\mathrm{s}}$ on labeled data only (*S*), model trained using segmentation loss with spatial transformation consistency regularization $L_{\mathrm{sup}} + \lambda L_{\mathrm{s}}$ on both labeled and unlabeled data (*S+*), and model trained using segmentation loss with spatial and temporal consistency regularization $L_{\mathrm{sup}} + \lambda_1 L_{\mathrm{s}} + \lambda_2 L_{\mathrm{t}}$ on both labeled and unlabeled data (*S+T*).

We also compare our consistency regularization method with two representative semi-supervised learning methods: mean teacher [18] and self-training [21]. In mean teacher, we implement the model using a similar Siamese student teacher architecture where student model is supervised to be consistent with the teacher model. However, we do not ask the model to be invariant or equivariant to image transformations. In self-training, we first train the segmentation model using labeled dataset and impute segmentations of the unlabeled images using the prediction of this model. We then train a second model using this augmented dataset. We compare these three methods using both full and partial datasets. To create partial dataset, we randomly sub-sample training and validation dataset to contain $5, 10, 20, 40, 60$ subjects while subjects in the test set remain the same.

3.3   Evaluation

To evaluate segmentation accuracy, we measure the volume overlap between the predicted and ground truth segmentation of placenta using the Dice similarity coefficient. We refer to this metric as Dice w. ground truth. In addition, we assess the consistency of our predictions across time. We apply our model to all volumes in the time series and measure the consistency of consecutive predictions using Dice similarity. We refer to this metric as temporal Dice. While we do not

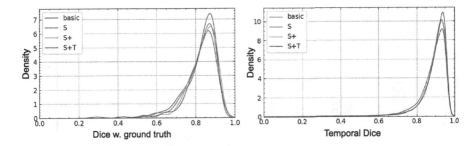

Fig. 2. Kernel Density Estimation of Dice Distribution of Four Training Settings. Left: Kernel density estimation of Dice w. ground truth for *Basic, S, S+,* and *S+T* settings. Right: Kernel density estimation of Temporal Dice from the same four training settings. In both metrics, we observe a tighter mode and a narrower long-tail distribution after applying our consistency regularization loss.

Table 1. Sample-wise Increase of Dice Score among Different Groups. We report the median (IQR) increase in Dice score relative to the *Basic* setting. We observe a moderate increase of Dice scores for ALL subjects, and large increase of Dice score for the LOW group.

	Dice w. ground truth			Temporal Dice		
	LOW	HIGH	ALL	LOW	HIGH	ALL
S vs. Basic	0.015±0.06	0.0060±0.02	0.008±0.03	0.060±0.19	0.003±0.03	0.003±0.03
S+ vs. Basic	0.022±0.06	0.0072±0.02	0.010±0.03	0.050±0.19	0.003±0.03	0.004±0.03
S+T vs. Basic	**0.027±0.05**	**0.0073±0.02**	**0.011±0.03**	**0.109±0.19**	**0.004±0.03**	**0.005±0.03**

expect perfect alignment in the presence of motion, relatively small motion of the placenta should yield a rough agreement. Thus, consecutive frames with low volume overlap are suggestive of segmentation errors. This provides a way to evaluate the segmentation quality without the excessive overhead of manual segmentation of the whole series. We also divide subjects into LOW and HIGH groups and report the Dice w. ground truth and temporal Dice per group. The HIGH group is defined as subjects whose performances are above threshold α in *Basic* training; LOW group is defined as those below. The performance in LOW group represents outliers and hard samples. We used $\alpha = 0.8$ for Dice w. ground truth and $\alpha = 0.7$ for temporal Dice.

We use cross-validation to select the best hyperparameters. We randomly divide the subjects into five folds. We then train the model on four folds and evaluate the model on the remaining fold. We repeat this process five times and report the mean and standard deviation of the performance across all subjects. We used the same hyperparameters for all the folds. The unlabeled training data is collected from the same participants in the labeled training data to ensure no overlapping subjects between training and testing.

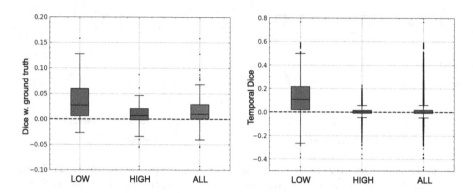

Fig. 3. Boxplots of Dice w. ground truth and temporal Dice among three groups. For S+T vs. Basic setting, we show boxplots of Dice w. ground truth and temporal Dice among LOW, HIGH, and ALL groups. We observe larger improvements in both metrics in LOW group.

3.4   Results

Figure 2 presents the Dice distribution of models trained with four different settings. After applying consistency regularization, we observe a tighter mode and a narrower long-tail distribution. Table 1 reports sample-wise improvement in volume overlap relative to the *Basic* for LOW, HIGH, and ALL groups. Our method provides moderate improvement for both groups and metrics (volume overlap with ground truth and agreement in consecutive frames). The improvement is more pronounced for LOW group. In Fig. 3, we visualize the Dice improvement of *S+T* relative to *Basic* among three groups. The improvement in the LOW group is significantly higher than that in the HIGH and ALL groups. This indicates that our method improves the robustness for outlier and hard samples. We also visualize several predictions from our model in Fig. 4.

Table 2 compares our approach to the mean teacher and self-training models. Our method outperforms mean teacher training strategy and self-training.

Table 2. Comparison between consistency regularization and other baseline SSL methods in both full and partial dataset settings.

Method	all	60	40	20	10	5
mean teacher	0.80±0.09	0.79±0.07	0.78±0.08	0.72±0.13	0.55±0.21	0.40±0.19
self-training	0.82±0.09	0.80±0.07	0.78±0.08	0.70±0.10	0.56±0.21	0.35±0.25
ours	0.84±0.07	0.82±0.08	0.79±0.08	0.73±0.12	0.53±0.20	0.39±0.23

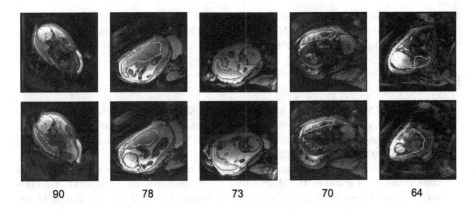

Fig. 4. Example Predictions of Five Subjects across Different Test Performance Yellow indicates ground truth segmentation and red indicates predictions. Each column represents the same subject. Top and bottom slices are 18mm apart. On the bottom is the Dice score of the entire image. (Color figure online)

4 Limitations and Future Work

There are several limitations to this study. First, our unlabeled samples are highly correlated with the labeled samples. This contradicts the typical semi-supervised learning assumption where unlabeled samples are drawn independently from the same distribution as the labeled samples. This partly explains our experimental results where using unlabeled samples introduced relatively small improvements. Future studies should include images from new subjects. Second, we did not register the images before applying temporal consistency loss. A more principled way to account for the differences between frames in the time series would include alignment before evaluating segmentation consistency. Future work should explore the integration of image registration in temporal consistency. Last, several novel loss functions to improve segmentation in fetal MRI have been proposed recently [2,13,20]. We did not study how our consistency regularization method interacts with these methods.

5 Conclusions

This work demonstrated a novel consistency regularization method that improves the performance and robustness of placenta segmentation in EPI MRI time series. The consistency regularization loss explicitly encourages the model to be consistent between transformations of the same image and between nearby frames in the time series. The evaluation shows that the method improves the overall segmentation accuracy and provides better performance for outlier and hard samples. Our method also improves the temporal coherency of the prediction. This could support the study of placenta and ultimately lead to more accurate placental biomarkers.

Acknowledgements. This research is supported by NIH NIBIB NAC P41EB015902, NIH NICHD R01HD100009, and NIH NIBIB 5R01EB032708, and the Swiss National Science Foundation project P500PT-206955.

References

1. Abulnaga, S.M., Abaci Turk, E., Bessmeltsev, M., Grant, P.E., Solomon, J., Golland, P.: Placental flattening via volumetric parameterization. In: Shen, D., et al. (eds.) MICCAI 2019. LNCS, vol. 11767, pp. 39–47. Springer, Cham (2019). https://doi.org/10.1007/978-3-030-32251-9_5
2. Abulnaga, S.M., et al.: Automatic segmentation of the placenta in BOLD MRI time series. In: Licandro, R., Melbourne, A., Abaci Turk, E., Macgowan, C., Hutter, J. (eds.) International Workshop on Preterm, Perinatal and Paediatric Image Analysis, vol. 13575, pp. 1–12. Springer, Cham (2022). https://doi.org/10.1007/978-3-031-17117-8_1
3. Alansary, A., et al.: Fast fully automatic segmentation of the human placenta from motion corrupted MRI. In: Ourselin, S., Joskowicz, L., Sabuncu, M.R., Unal, G., Wells, W. (eds.) MICCAI 2016. LNCS, vol. 9901, pp. 589–597. Springer, Cham (2016). https://doi.org/10.1007/978-3-319-46723-8_68
4. Baur, C., Albarqouni, S., Navab, N.: Semi-supervised deep learning for fully convolutional networks. In: Descoteaux, M., Maier-Hein, L., Franz, A., Jannin, P., Collins, D., Duchesne, S. (eds.) Medical Image Computing and Computer Assisted Intervention - MICCAI 2017: 20th International Conference, Quebec City, QC, Canada, 11–13 September 2017, Proceedings, Part III 20, vol. 10435, pp. 311–319. Springer, Cham (2017). https://doi.org/10.1007/978-3-319-66179-7_36
5. Bertinetto, L., Valmadre, J., Henriques, J.F., Vedaldi, A., Torr, P.H.: Fully-convolutional Siamese networks for object tracking. In: Hua, G., Jégou, H. (eds.) Computer Vision-ECCV 2016 Workshops: Amsterdam, The Netherlands, 8–10 October and 15–16 October 2016, Proceedings, Part II 14, vol. 9914, pp. 850–865. Springer, Cham (2016). https://doi.org/10.1007/978-3-319-48881-3_56
6. Chen, X., He, K.: Exploring simple Siamese representation learning. In: Proceedings of the IEEE/CVF Conference on Computer Vision and Pattern Recognition, pp. 15750–15758 (2021)
7. Chicco, D.: Siamese neural networks: an overview. In: Artificial Neural Networks, pp. 73–94 (2021)
8. Cui, W., et al.: Semi-supervised brain lesion segmentation with an adapted mean teacher model. In: Chung, A., Gee, J., Yushkevich, P., Bao, S. (eds.) Information Processing in Medical Imaging: 26th International Conference, IPMI 2019, Hong Kong, China, 2–7 June 2019, Proceedings 26, vol. 11492, pp. 554–565. Springer, Cham (2019). https://doi.org/10.1007/978-3-030-20351-1_43
9. Kamnitsas, K., et al.: Unsupervised domain adaptation in brain lesion segmentation with adversarial networks. In: Niethammer, M., et al. (eds.) Information Processing in Medical Imaging: 25th International Conference, IPMI 2017, Boone, NC, USA, 25–30 June 2017, Proceedings 25, vol. 10265, pp. 597–609. Springer, Cham (2017). https://doi.org/10.1007/978-3-319-59050-9_47
10. Kingma, D.P., Ba, J.: Adam: a method for stochastic optimization. arXiv preprint arXiv:1412.6980 (2014)
11. León, R.L., Li, K.T., Brown, B.P.: A retrospective segmentation analysis of placental volume by magnetic resonance imaging from first trimester to term gestation. Pediatr. Radiol. **48**(13), 1936–1944 (2018)

12. Li, X., Yu, L., Chen, H., Fu, C.W., Xing, L., Heng, P.A.: Transformation-consistent self-ensembling model for semisupervised medical image segmentation. IEEE Trans. Neural Networks Learn. Syst. **32**(2), 523–534 (2020)

13. Ren, M., Dey, N., Styner, M., Botteron, K., Gerig, G.: Local spatiotemporal representation learning for longitudinally-consistent neuroimage analysis. Adv. Neural. Inf. Process. Syst. **35**, 13541–13556 (2022)

14. Ronneberger, O., Fischer, P., Brox, T.: U-Net: convolutional networks for biomedical image segmentation. In: Navab, N., Hornegger, J., Wells, W., Frangi, A. (eds.) Medical Image Computing and Computer-Assisted Intervention - MICCAI 2015, vol. 9351, pp. 234–241. Springer, Cham (2015). https://doi.org/10.1007/978-3-319-24574-4_28

15. Sokloska, M., et al.: Placental image analysis using coupled diffusion-weighted and multi-echo T2 MRI and a multi-compartment model. In: MICCAI Workshop on Perinatal, Preterm and Paediatric Image Analysis (PIPPI) (2016)

16. Taleb, A., et al.: 3D self-supervised methods for medical imaging. Adv. Neural. Inf. Process. Syst. **33**, 18158–18172 (2020)

17. Tang, Y., et al.: Self-supervised pre-training of Swin transformers for 3D medical image analysis. In: Proceedings of the IEEE/CVF Conference on Computer Vision and Pattern Recognition, pp. 20730–20740 (2022)

18. Tarvainen, A., Valpola, H.: Mean teachers are better role models: weight-averaged consistency targets improve semi-supervised deep learning results. In: Advances in Neural Information Processing Systems, vol. 30 (2017)

19. Xia, J., He, Y., Yin, X., Han, S., Gu, X.: Direct-product volumetric parameterization of handlebodies via harmonic fields. In: Shape Modeling International Conference, pp. 3–12. IEEE (2010)

20. Xu, J., et al.: Semi-supervised learning for fetal brain MRI quality assessment with ROI consistency. In: Martel, A.L., et al. (eds.) Medical Image Computing and Computer Assisted Intervention-MICCAI 2020: 23rd International Conference, Lima, Peru, 4–8 October 2020, Proceedings, Part VI 23, vol. 12266, pp. 386–395. Springer, Cham (2020). https://doi.org/10.1007/978-3-030-59725-2_37

21. Yarowsky, D.: Unsupervised word sense disambiguation rivaling supervised methods. In: 33rd Annual Meeting of the Association for Computational Linguistics, pp. 189–196 (1995)

Visualization and Quantification of Placental Vasculature Using MRI

Joanna Chappell[1,5]($\boxtimes$), Magdalena Sokolska[2,5], Rosalind Aughwane[3,5], Alys R. Clark[4,5], Sebastien Ourselin[1,5], Anna L. David[3,4,5], and Andrew Melbourne[1,5]

[1] School of Biomedical Engineering and Imaging Sciences (BMEIS), King's College London, London, UK
Joanna.Chappell@kcl.ac.uk
[2] Department of Medical Physics and Biomedical Engineering, University College London Hospitals, London, UK
[3] Elizabeth Garrett Anderson Institute for Women's Health, University College, London, UK
[4] Auckland Bioengineering Institute, Auckland, New Zealand
[5] University College London Hospital NHS Foundation Trust, London, UK

Abstract. Visualization of the placental vasculature in vivo is important for parameterization of placental function which is related to obstetric pathologies such as fetal growth restriction (FGR). However, most analysis of this vasculature is conducted ex vivo after delivery of the placenta. The aim of this study was to determine whether in vivo MRI imaging can accurately quantify the feto-placental vasculature, and to determine the impact of MRI contrast on its identification. Six different MRI contrasts were compared across 10 different cases. Image quality metrics were calculated, and analysis of vasculature segmentations performed. Measures of assessment included the vessel radius distribution, vessel connectivity and the identification of vessel loops. T_2 HASTE imaging performed the best both qualitatively, and quantitatively for PSNR and connectivity measures. A larger number of segmented branches at the smallest radii were observed, indicative of a richer description of the in vivo vascular tree. These were then mapped to MR perfusion fraction measurements from intra-voxel incoherent motion (IVIM) MRI. Mapped results were compared to measures extracted from gold-standard ex vivo micro-CT of the placenta and showed similar vessel density patterns suggesting that placental vessel analysis may be feasible in vivo.

Keywords: Placenta · Vasculature · Segmentation · Placental MRI

1 Introduction

Placental function with effective maternal-fetal oxygen and nutrient exchange is dependent on the development of a highly vascularized placental circulatory system. The placental vasculature is difficult to image in vivo with the majority of analyses in the literature completed ex vivo.

A well-functioning placenta is vital for healthy fetal growth and development. Many complications of pregnancy such as fetal growth restriction (FGR) and pre-eclampsia are

D. Link-Sourani et al. (Eds.): PIPPI 2023, LNCS 14246, pp. 88–97, 2023.
https://doi.org/10.1007/978-3-031-45544-5_8

linked to placental insufficiency and inadequate vasculogenesis and angiogenesis. FGR in the UK leads to 2/3 of stillbirths [1] and earlier clinical knowledge of the placental function would aid in clinical decision making. In FGR placentas, there appears to be reduced vascular branching and narrower vessels leading to a significant reduction in uteroplacental blood flow and hence oxygen and nutrient exchange [2].

Ultrasound is the most utilized imaging technique during pregnancy, providing a low cost and accessible option, able to assess the uteroplacental blood flow and fetal vascular impedance [3]. However, MRI has been increasingly used to investigate pregnancy complications, and can measure variations in the placental structure as well as provide blood and oxygenation metrics [1, 4].

Placental vasculature modelling is not a new concept and has been completed across vascular scales utilizing different imaging methods. Differences in the placental vasculature have been observed ex vivo using micro-CT [5] and at the microstructural level using confocal laser scanning [6]. Evidence suggests that placental vasculature does change ex vivo with the cessation of uteroplacental blood circulation [2]. Additionally, ex vivo imaging does not provide immediate information for patient specific decision making.

MRI provides a solution to this, by segmenting the vasculature trees in combination with diffusion and relaxation-based perfusion and oxygenation measurements. However, visualization of blood vessels using MRI is difficult and can vary with different MRI contrasts. This study aims to assess the feasibility of extracting placental vasculatures from in vivo MRI, using different contrasts, and to quantify the nature of vascular networks extracted from this in vivo imaging.

1.1 MRI Acquisitions and Differing Contrasts

Relaxation times (T_1 and T_2) describe how long the tissue takes to return to equilibrium after a radiofrequency (RF) pulse. T_1 and T_2 depend on different tissues. Fluids have long T_1 (1500–2000 ms), water-based tissues are usually mid-range (400–1200 ms) and fat tissues are usually short (100–150 ms). In general, images have contrast which depends on proton density, T_1 or T_2. The T_1 weighted MRI enhances the appearance of fatty tissue, while T_2-weighted images enhance the signal of the water [7]. T_2* is the transversal relaxation time constant within gradient-echo MRI using a long repetition time, long echo time and low flip angle, which can be used for detecting changes in oxygen saturation [8].

MRI HASTE (Half-Fourier Acquisition Single-shot Turbo Spin Echo) is a rapid imaging technique to acquire T_2-weighted images, utilizing a single-shot acquisition and half-Fourier sampling to reduce acquisition time. It is particularly useful in maternal and fetal MRI due to its fast acquisition time reducing the effect of fetal motion [9].

Diffusion-weighted imaging (DWI) is common in medical MRI and particularly in placental imaging measuring the displacement of the water molecules within the tissue over a time interval. The diffusion sensitivity can be characterized by the b-value, which reflects the strength and timing of the gradients used to create the DWIs [10].

Intravoxel incoherent motion (IVIM) MRI is an imaging method to separate the vascular and nonvascular components of the anatomy. IVIM measures the microcirculation in the capillary bed and has shown sensitivity to multiple pregnancy complications with fetal and maternal origins including FGR [11]. In this way IVIM measurements can provide a measurement of vascular density within the placenta, even when the vessel network is not resolvable (Fig. 1.).

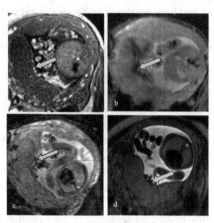

Fig. 1. The figure shows the different MRI contrast images for a pregnancy FGR. Shown are (a) T_1, (b) T_2^*, (c) IVIM (at b-value $= 0$ s/mm^2), and (d) HASTE. Major blood vessels are identified by arrows. A visual difference in the appearance of the vasculature can be observed.

2   Methods

2.1   Data Acquisition

MRI data from 10 pregnant patients (6 with FGR (estimated fetal weight $< 10^{th}$ centile) and 4 normally grown fetuses) at $24 + 2$–$33 + 6$ GA was acquired with a 1.5T Siemens Avanto under free-breathing [12]. The voxel resolution was $1.9 \times 1.9 \times 6$ mm. The data was acquired as a combination of 7 b-values and 9 echo-times. IVIM was acquired at b-values (0,50,100,150,200,400,600 s/mm^2) and T_2 relaxometry at echo times (77, 90, 120, 150, 180, 210, 240, 270, 300 ms). To allow T_2 fitting, all echo times were acquired at b-value 0 and all b-values at 96 ms. In addition, data were acquired at b-values 50 and 200 for t $= 81$, 90, 120, 150,180, 210 and 240 ms. The total acquisition time was approximately 20 min making the data acquisition tolerable for subjects. This integrated acquisition provides an improved separation of long T2 compartments with different incoherent motion properties which integrate the effects of diffusion, perfusion and oxygenation [13]. The study was approved by the UK National Research Ethics Service and all participants gave written informed consent (London – Hampstead Research Ethics Committee, REC reference 15/LO/1488). All the data were anonymized. All patients had T_1 and HASTE contrasts, 6 had T_2^*, 3 had additional T_2 HASTE and 3 had additional IVIM diffusion imaging.

2.2 Image Quantification Metrics

Images were quantified with the following measures:

Signal-to-Noise Ratio (SNR). Measured by taking the mean of a high-intensity region of interest and dividing by the standard deviation of the region of noise outside of the imaged object [14].

Peak Signal-to-Noise Ratio (PSNR). Is an expression of the ratio between the maximum values of signal and the power of the distorting noise that affects the quality of the image, it is calculated as [14].

$$\text{PSNR} = 20 \log_{10}\left(\frac{MAX_f}{\sqrt{MSE}}\right),$$

where MAX_f is the maximum signal and MSE is the mean squared error.

Structural Similarity Image Metric (SSIM) measures the local structural similarity, by using a correlation between the quality and the perception of the human visual system. Instead of using traditional error summation methods, the SSIM models image distortion and contrast distortion [14].

Entropy is a statistical measure of the randomness that can be used to characterize the texture of the input image. It is a quantitative measure of the information transmitted in the image. It is defined as:

Entropy $= -\sum_{i=1}^{n} p \bullet \log_2 p$

where p contains the normalized histogram counts [15]–[17].

2.3 Quantification of Vessel Segmentation

Manual segmentations of the vessel trees were carried out on each image contrast and the resultant vascular tree quantified using:

Maximum and Minimum Radii from the manual segmentations were calculated alongside the volume of vessels segmented. These were plotted against each of the contrasts and visualized in 3D using VesselVio [18].

Connectivity of the segmentations was quantified using skeletonization; the branch points and vessel lengths were calculated. From this the connectivity index was assessed as total length of the vessel network divided by the total area of the segmentation. The higher the connectivity index the more interconnected the vessels are within the segmentation [19].

Looping of the segmentations was quantified by detecting the connected components in a closed or distinct loop [20].

2.4 Statistics

The difference between each metric described in Sect. 2.3 and 2.4 that was derived from each MRI contrast was assessed statistically using using a 2 tailed t-test with a p value of < 0.05 defined as statistically significant.

2.5 Segmentation Performance Evaluation

In order to evaluate the manual segmentations, we compare them to properties of the fetal vasculature from a gold standard ex vivo perfused placenta that had undergone micro-CT examination. Data from a single placenta was acquired from a woman undergoing elective term caesarean section following uncomplicated pregnancy. The placenta was perfused with Microfil and imaged over the whole volume via micro-CT with isotropic voxel size of 116.5 μm [2]. The placental vasculature was extracted and analyzed using the same analysis as for the MRI [5].

The MRI and CT vessel segmentations and networks were analyzed. The vessel trees from the HASTE MRI and micro-CT were skeletonized and vessel endpoints extracted. The local vessel density was then measured distal to each endpoint. In the case of MRI, vessel density is estimated from IVIM-MRI weighted by a Gaussian distribution from each skeleton endpoint with a 3 pixels standard deviation. The distance of each endpoint from the umbilical cord insertion point is measured. In the case of the micro-CT, the vessel segmentation is thresholded at a vessel radius corresponding to the start of the placental stem arteries. Subsequently the local vessel density is measured at each of these end-points. Vessel density is estimated as the volume of segmented vessel in a region close to the corresponding endpoint, with 2.5 pixels radius. Distances of each end-point from the umbilical cord insertion are measured. A comparison was made between the results of the MRI and micro-CT vessel density measurements and how they vary with distance from cord insertion.

3 Results

Figure 2 shows the vessel segmentations obtained for each of the imaging contrasts for one case, the segmentation quantification of the radii and volume is stated.

Figure 3 shows how the distribution of radii from each of the segmentations varies between imaging contrasts.

Values for the four image quality metrics are shown in Table 1. Only the PSNR was significant between the diffusion IVIM imaging and the HASTE imaging. The volume of vessels identified was higher for the IVIM imaging, the connectivity was significantly higher for the HASTE imaging than the IVIM, T_1 and T_2^*. Identified looping increased with increased connectivity.

3.1 Validation from Micro-CT

Figure 4 compares image segmentations from MRI and micro-CT and Fig. 5 shows the relationship between vessel density and distance from umbilical insertion point. Both MRI data and micro-CT data show a significant negative trend of vessel density with distance. The agreement between these two datatypes is consistent with previous ex vivo literature and demonstrates that MRI can extract comparable relationships in vivo by the combination of high-resolution structural imaging and IVIM imaging.

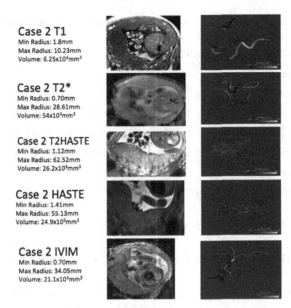

Case 2 T1
Min Radius: 1.8mm
Max Radius: 10.23mm
Volume: 6.25x10³mm³

Case 2 T2*
Min Radius: 0.70mm
Max Radius: 28.61mm
Volume: 54x10³mm³

Case 2 T2HASTE
Min Radius: 1.12mm
Max Radius: 62.52mm
Volume: 26.2x10³mm³

Case 2 HASTE
Min Radius: 1.41mm
Max Radius: 55.13mm
Volume: 24.9x10³mm³

Case 2 IVIM
Min Radius: 0.70mm
Max Radius: 34.05mm
Volume: 21.1x10³mm³

Fig. 2. The contrast comparison for the visualization of the vessels alongside the 3D model of the segmented vessels from VesselVio. Maximum (Max) and minimum (Min) radii of identified vessels, as well as total volume of vessels is stated. Colorbars represent vessel radius.

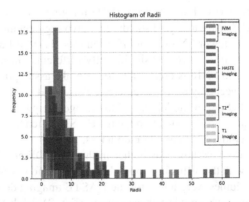

Fig. 3. The spread and the histogram of the radii showing the density spread for each of the contrasts for all the cases and across all of the image contrasts.

4 Discussion

This work has shown that compared with other MRI protocols T_2 HASTE images provide a better visualization of the feto-placental vasculature, with the quantitative measures for PSNR and connectivity being significantly higher than the other contrasts. Vessel segmentations can be combined with IVIM MRI data to allow a coupled analysis of vessel density. Validation with ex vivo Micro-CT data showed that coupled segmentations from

Table 1. Combined results from the image quality metrics and the segmentation properties

	HASTE	T$_2$ HASTE	T$_1$	T$_2$*	IVIM
Image Quality Metrics					
PSNR	30.9 ± 0.79	29.2 ± 2.13	39.9 ± 0.79	37.5 ± 2.13	42 ± 1.77
SNR	19.9 ± 0.010	20.0 ± 0.010	19.9 ± 0.026	20.0 ± 0.030	20.0 ± 0.040
Entropy	6.72 ± 0.003	6.72 ± 0.002	6.72 ± 0.004	6.72 ± 0.005	6.71 ± 0.006
SSIM	0.09 ± 0.0002	0.09 ± 0.0002	0.09 ± 0.0005	0.09 ± 0.0006	0.09 ± 0.0006
Segmentation Properties					
Volume (mm^3)	9596.60	26210.68	10578.8	34825.5592	55050.9
Max Radius (mm)	44.41 ± 13.78	56.3 ± 8.803	17.84 ± 14.8	18.6 ± 6.88	28.45 ± 10.2
Min Radius (mm)	1.41 ± 0.46	1.81 ± 0.98	1.06 ± 0.54	0.707 ± 0.23	1.81 ± 0.50
Connectivity	49.36 ± 3.96	56.03 ± 6.94	40.03 ± 6.57	51.34 ± 6.94	41.05 ± 4.33
Looping	25 ± 14.5	48.5 ± 16.3	8 ± 2	11.5 ± 2.5	6 ± 2

HASTE and markers of vessel density from IVIM imaging show similar spatial trends in terms of the vessel density to a gold standard ex vivo segmentation.

HASTE cases have lower PNSR than diffusion models (IVIM and DECIDE). The other image quality metrics were not significantly different. There are limitations to the use of the PSNR and SNR as both calculations make assumptions as to the image intensity reducing the accuracy of the parameters. This could be due to the SSIM being correlated with the HVS color model and all the images being greyscale. The entropy values were very similar throughout, although the HASTE often had the lowest standard deviation, implying a reduced apparent randomness.

The segmented vessel volume was higher in the DECIDE and IVIM cases, likely related to the PSNR, with the diffusion models being lower and vasculature being harder to observe clearly. Volumes were lower for the HASTE imaging despite visual appearance of more branching observed in these images (Fig. 2). With HASTE imaging, a higher number of branching units can be observed (Fig. 2 and 3) with radii distributions with higher median and larger numbers of smaller vessels than any other contrast. The connectivity of the segmentations calculated for the T$_2$ imaging, HASTE and star, gave the highest values with the T$_1$ imaging and diffusion imaging having similar averages.

Vessel looping was highest in the HASTE contrasts most likely due to greater value of branching segments in comparison to the T$_1$ and the diffusion imaging. The connectivity and lopping parameters correlated positively as more branches led to higher looping. However, the looping could be more accurately detected using a cycle detection algorithms like depth-first search (DFS) or Tarjan's algorithm.

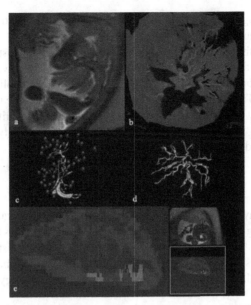

Fig. 4. Comparison of vasculature segmentations from MRI and Micro-CT: Sagittal slice from HASTE MRI with the segmentation of the vasculature overlayed in red (A), Micro-CT with the segmented vasculature in red (B). 3D skeletons of the segmentations in green with the red endpoints for the MRI and Micro-CT respectively (C and D). IVIM perfusion density map, with end point locations identified in red, segmentation in green and skeleton in blue (E).

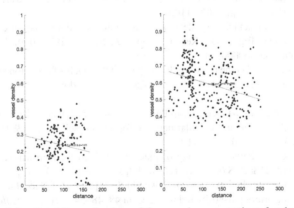

Fig. 5. The vessel density at the end points of the vessel segmentations for the MRI on the left and micro-CT data on the right.

One limitation of these measures is that they are an incomplete assessment of the quality of the imaging and the quality of the resulting segmentation. The manual segmentations are possibly limited by user-error, and are subjective, but were required in this study to ensure vascular connectivity. However, in combination, the vessel segmentation and image quality measures have the potential to be combined to form a unified cost-function of image quality and vessel extraction. This may eventually help automate the vessel segmentation process.

Comparison with micro-CT data showing vessel density against distance from the umbilical cord insertion for MRI and ex vivo micro-CT (Fig. 5) indicates that both show a negative correlation. This result is comparable to previously published ex vivo work in the placenta [2]. The correlation is not as strong in the MRI as the resolution of vessel branching is greatly reduced due to a reduced resolution and quality of segmentation but the substitution of vessel density with IVIM perfusion density allows sub-voxel inferences to be made.

5   Conclusion

In conclusion, we have shown that feto-placental vascular networks can be extracted from in vivo MRI imaging data. Comparison with micro-CT data indicates that it is possible to obtain in vivo MRI data that with correspondence to subsequent post-delivery analysis. Our findings suggest that more detailed placental analysis may be possible in vivo, supporting the translation of advanced placental imaging technology to the clinic.

References

1. Aughwane, R., et al.: Placental MRI and its application to fetal intervention. Prenat. Diagn. **40**(1), 38–48 (2020). https://doi.org/10.1002/pd.5526
2. Byrne, M., et al.: Structure-function relationships in the feto-placental circulation from in silico interpretation of micro-CT vascular structures. J. Theor. Biol. **517**, 110630 (2021). https://doi.org/10.1016/j.jtbi.2021.110630
3. Turk, E.A., et al.: Placental MRI: developing accurate quantitative measures of oxygenation HHS public access. Top. Magn. Reson. Imaging **28**(5), 285–297 (2019). https://doi.org/10.1097/RMR.0000000000000221
4. Melbourne, A., et al.: On the use of multicompartment models of diffusion and relaxation for placental imaging. Placenta **112**, 197–203 (2021). https://doi.org/10.1016/j.placenta.2021.07.302
5. Tun, W.M.: Differences in placental capillary shear stress in fetal growth restriction may affect endothelial cell function and vascular network formation. Sci. Reports **9**(1), (2019). https://doi.org/10.1038/s41598-019-46151-6
6. Burton, G.J., et al.: Pathophysiology of placental-derived fetal growth restriction. Am. J. Obstet. Gynecol. **218**(2), S745–S761 (2018). https://doi.org/10.1016/j.ajog.2017.11.577
7. Sinding, M., et al.: Prediction of low birth weight: Comparison of placental T2* estimated by MRI and uterine artery pulsatility index. Placenta **49**, 48–54 (2017). https://doi.org/10.1016/J.PLACENTA.2016.11.009
8. Kawahara, D., et al.: T1-weighted and T2-weighted MRI image synthesis with convolutional generative adversarial networks. Reports Pract. Oncol. Radiother. **26**(1), 35–42 (2021). https://doi.org/10.5603/RPOR.a2021.0005
9. Semelka, R.C., et al.: HASTE MR imaging: description of technique and preliminary results in the abdomen. J. Magnet. Resonance Imag. **6**(4), 698–699 (1996). https://doi.org/10.1002/jmri.1880060420
10. Fusco, R., et al.: A comparison of fitting algorithms for diffusion-weighted MRI data analysis using an intravoxel incoherent motion model. Magn Reson Mater Phy **30**, 113–120 (2017). https://doi.org/10.1007/s10334-016-0591-y

11. Liao, Y., et al.: "Journal pre-proof detecting abnormal placental microvascular flow in maternal and fetal diseases based on flow-compensated and non-compensated intravoxel incoherent motion imaging", p. Placenta (2022). https://doi.org/10.1016/j.placenta.2022.01.010
12. Aughwane, R., et al.: Magnetic resonance imaging measurement of placental perfusion and oxygen saturation in early-onset fetal growth restriction. Int. J. Obstet. Gynaecol. **128**(2), 337-345 (2021). https://doi.org/10.1111/1471-0528.16459
13. Melbourne, A., et al.: Separating fetal and maternal placenta circulations using multiparametric MRI (2016). https://www.researchgate.net/publication/324079328
14. Plenge, E., et al.: LNCS 8151 - Super-Resolution Reconstruction Using Cross-Scale Self-similarity in Multi-slice MRI (2013). http://www.bigr.nl/
15. Ji, Q., et al.: A novel, fast entropy-minimization algorithm for bias field correction in MR images.
16. Obuchowicz, R., et al.: Magnetic resonance image quality assessment by using non-maximum suppression and entropy analysis. Entropy **22**(2), 220 (2020). https://doi.org/10.3390/e22020220
17. Tsai, D.Y., et al.: Information entropy measure for evaluation of image quality. J. Digit. Imaging **21**(3), 338–347 (2008). https://doi.org/10.1007/s10278-007-9044-5
18. Bumgarner, J.R., et al.: Open-source analysis and visualization of segmented vasculature datasets with VesselVio. Cell Reports Methods **2**(4), 100189 (2022). https://doi.org/10.1016/j.crmeth.2022.100189
19. Zhang, J., et al.: Techniques and algorithms for hepatic vessel skeletonization in medical images: a survey. Entropy **24**(4), 465 (2022). https://doi.org/10.3390/e24040465
20. Li, K., et al.: Optimal surface segmentation in volumetric images - A graph-theoretic approach. IEEE Trans. Pattern Anal. Mach. Intell. **28**(1), 119–134 (2006). https://doi.org/10.1109/TPAMI.2006.19

The Comparison Analysis of the Cervical Features Between Second-and Third-Trimester Pregnancy in Ultrasound Images Using eXplainable AI

Yeong-Eun Jeon[1], Ga-Hyun Son[2], Ho-Jung Kim[1], Jae-Jun Lee[3], and Dong-Ok Won[1,4(✉)]

[1] Department of Artificial Intelligence Convergence, Hallym University, Chuncheon, Korea
{M22056,hojungkim,dongok.won}@hallym.ac.kr

[2] Department of Obstetrics and Gynecology Medicine, College of Medicine, Hallym University, Chuncheon, Korea
gahyuns@hallym.or.kr

[3] Department of Anesthesiology and Pain Medicine, College of Medicine, Hallym University, Chuncheon, Korea
iloveu59@hallym.or.kr

[4] College of Medicine, Hallym University, Chuncheon, Korea

Abstract. The fetus is maintained in the uterus by the cervix throughout pregnancy. In the last period of pregnancy, the cervix softens, shortens, and expands in preparation for labor. When most clinicians check for changes in the cervix, like softness, they use palpation. However, since this palpation causes discomfort to the mother, we want to compare the status of the area around the cervical canal according to the pregnancy period through ultrasound images only. Therefore, we trained the deep learning network model and obtained high performance for the second and third-trimester classifications. Further, we used explainable Artificial Intelligence (XAI) techniques (i.e., Grad-CAM/Grad-CAM++, Score-CAM, Eigen-CAM) in order to find which areas were important features during the deep learning network training. As a result, in the third-trimester period images, it was seen that the fetal head was a major feature, however, it was found that the cervix and cervical border were also affected without a fetal head. Also, it was determined that the classification in the second-trimester images was based on the potential region toward the lower uterus from the internal os. By analyzing the deep learning network result using the XAI approaches, this might be used as a new feature to describe the cervical change.

Keywords: Cervix · Pregnancy trimester · Explainable AI(XAI) · Deep learning · Ultrasound images

---

Y.-E. Jeon and G.-H. Son—These authors contributed equally to this work.

© The Author(s), under exclusive license to Springer Nature Switzerland AG 2023
D. Link-Sourani et al. (Eds.): PIPPI 2023, LNCS 14246, pp. 98–108, 2023.
https://doi.org/10.1007/978-3-031-45544-5_9

1   Introduction

The standard pregnancy lasts 40 weeks that begins on the first day of your last menstrual period. The pregnant phase can be divided into three main periods [18]. First-trimester pregnancy lasts up to 12 weeks, and second-trimester pregnancy lasts from 13 to 28 whole weeks, and the baby is growing rapidly at this time. The third trimester means 29–40 weeks of pregnancy. During the last trimester, the mother may experience contractions in which the muscles of the uterus tighten and changes occur in the cervix. The cervix is the segment of the canal that connects the vagina and uterus [13]. It supports the weight of the growing fetus and maintains the fetus in the uterus throughout pregnancy. Gradually closer to the end of pregnancy, the cervix softens, shortens, and expands for the fetus's birth [3,12]. In some researches [4,5,16,22], they studied the relation to cervical features in the perinatal period or labor. In addition, evaluation of changes in the cervix, such as the sonographic assessment of cervical length, is used as a predictor of preterm birth [17,23]. However, these changes, like softness in the cervix, are rather difficult to detect through ultrasound imaging. The clinicians usually used palpation to figure out cervical changes in the mother. This palpation not only causes discomfort to the mother but can also be a non-objective indicator since clinicians may have different standards for the degree of softness in the cervix. So, we want to identify the cervical features according to pregnancy trimester using only ultrasound images through a deep-learning neural network model. In this study, we aimed to compare cervical features according to the pregnancy period on ultrasound images. Further, we use the eXplainable Artificial Intelligence (XAI) methods that interpret the deep neural network model's output. It shows which area the model makes a decision based on.

2   Method

In the first part of this section, we discussed the explainable artificial intelligence tool based on Grad-CAM/Grad-CAM++, Score-CAM, and Eigen-CAM, which is used to interpret the features of the trained deep neural network model. Second, we presented deep neural network models such as ResNet, DenseNet, and EfficientNet that perform classification tasks. Finally, we described the dataset and pre-processing for ultrasound images.

2.1   eXplainable Artificial Intelligence(XAI) - CAM Based Methods

eXplainable Artificial Intelligence (XAI) means presenting the result of a model in a form that humans can understand [20]. Most of the approaches can be divided into two categories: CAM-based or Attribution propagation methods. Class Activation Map (CAM)-based methods [24] are based on activations or gradients in relation to each layer's input, similar to Grad-CAM [15]. Another approach is the attribution propagation method, which is defined by the Deep

Taylor Decomposition framework [10] such as the Layer-wise Relevance Propagation (LRP) method [1]. So, we selected CAM-based methods good at localization to interpret the results of a model trained on ultrasound images.

Grad-CAM and Grad-CAM++. Gradient Class Activation Map (Grad-CAM) provides a heatmap-based explanation of the deep neural network model outputs [15]. When it is combined with the model's feature map, the heatmap shows how important certain parts of the model's structure are to the result. In contrast to CAM, the structure of the model is not constrained, and there is no resolution loss due to the size of the feature map being the same as that of the input image. However, Grad-CAM has an issue with localization appearing in a small area. This affects classifying multiple objects and makes it difficult to obtain the results. Therefore, Grad-CAM++ [2] uses the weighted-sum method to calculate weights instead of Global Average Pooling (GAP) on Grad-CAM [15]. It is made to enable localization to occur in a specific location without getting crushed. This has the benefit of being localized over a larger area and can create a good saliency map for multiple objects.

Score-CAM. Existing CAM methods assume that the target score will increase with the weight of the activation map. However, the vast majority of the cases do not work as existing methods. So, Score-CAM creates a heatmap, with the importance determined by the difference between the baseline and the feature of each channel [21]. Also, since a heatmap can be generated without using a gradient, it is not affected by the gradient vanishing issue.

Eigen-CAM. Eigen-CAM is a method of generating a heatmap using the first eigenvector obtained through principal component analysis (PCA) in the learned weight matrix [11]. It shows how to localize objects well by generating heatmaps without having to change the network structure or calculate noisy gradients.

2.2 Deep Neural Network Model for Classification Task

ResNet. ResNet has consisted of the residual blocks, which have skip-connection [6]. In a plain network, the deeper the layer of the neural network, it occurs the gradient vanishing issue. So, it proposed a method that adds the input to the output value after some layers. This prevents image features from being lost when the model is trained with the deep neural network.

DenseNet. DenseNet is a model that can gain high performance with a small number of parameters by connecting feature maps of all layers [7]. By concatenating the feature maps of the previous layer with those of all subsequent layers, it may reduce gradient issues. Also, since information is not lost, the features can be reused.

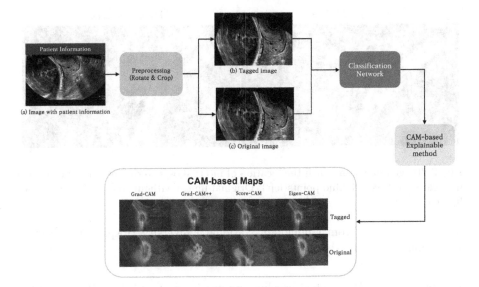

Fig. 1. The proposed framework in this research: It can be divided into two parts. The first stage is feature extraction and classification with a deep neural network, and the next is the interpretation stage using the eXplainable Artificial Intelligence (XAI) approach.

EfficientNet. We also selected EfficientNet [19], which improves the accuracy of models by changing the size of the input image and the depth and width of the model. In EfficientNet, which has the squeeze-and-excitation (SE) block, it only takes the most crucial information from each channel and decides how significant each channel is compared to the others.

2.3 Dataset and Preprocessing

The suggested framework for our research is shown in Fig. 1. First, deep neural networks such as ResNet, DenseNet, and EfficientNet are used for feature extraction and classification. The next step is the interpretation part using eXplainable AI with CAM-based methods.

Dataset. 1012 ultrasound images from 407 pregnant women between 37 and 41 weeks were collected at Hallym University Kangnam Sacred Heart Hospital (IRB No. 2023-06-007). 308 of these pregnant women overlapped in both classes. The data consisted of 681 s-trimester (16–24 weeks) pregnancies and 331 third-trimester(36–40 weeks) pregnancy classes. The ultrasound image contained information on the patient's age, the date of treatment, and the ultrasound equipment. Also, we obtained cervix marker images from medical experts hand-designed, in which the red and blue points represent the beginning and end points of the cervix, respectively (Fig. 2.). Additionally, we collected 160

(a) Tagged image   (b) Original image

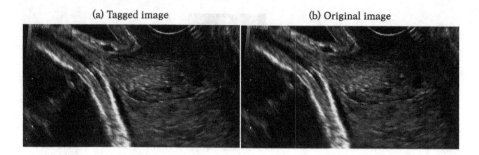

Fig. 2. Tagged image in which the location of internal os/external os was marked by a medical expert as red/blue points(left), Original image without markers(right) (Color figure online)

ultrasound images from Chungnam National University Hospital for external validation.

Preprocessing. We applied baseline pre-processing to all data. It consisted of rotation and cropping. We need to adjust the images to include the cervical canal location in the training data to figure out the differences in the cervical features during the pregnancy period. So, we calculated the angle between the red and blue points, the beginning and the end of the cervix, in ultrasound images. We rotated images at a calculated angle to align two points parallel. After rotating, the images were cropped to a size of 550 by 300 pixels based on the red point in the cervix marker images.

2.4   Experimental Design

The ratio used to divide the training and evaluation datasets was 8:2. In order to solve the problem of data imbalance, we also conducted data augmentation such as horizontal flip and gaussian noise. We used ResNet-101, DenseNet-121, and EfficientNet-b7 as feature extraction backbone networks and additional fully-connected layers with dropout as classifiers. The performance of models was optimized with Adam optimizer, learning rate of 0.0001, dropout of 0.4, and weight decay of 0.001. After obtaining the results for each model, the CAM-based method was applied to each of the tagged images with the cervical marker and the original image without them.

3   Results

3.1   Comparison of Heatmap Between Second- And Third-Trimester

In Table 1, each deep neural network model achieved a high AUC score of over 90% as a result of classification in the second and third-trimester pregnancy. Also, Fig. 3. shows a heatmap for each class showing which areas were significant

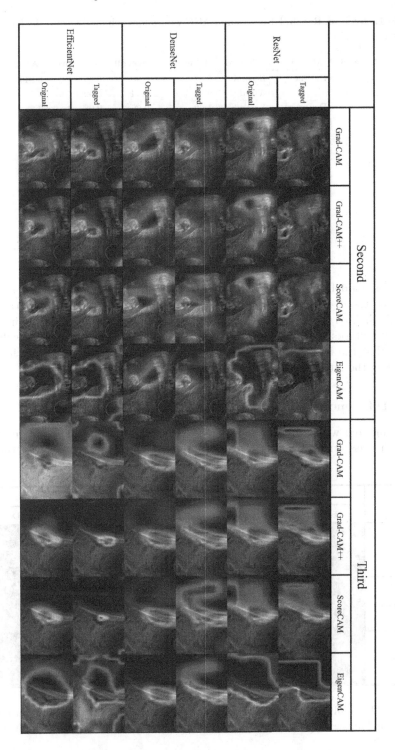

Fig. 3. The result of the heatmap for Second- and Third-trimester classes on the same ultrasound image according to XAI methods for each classification model: ResNet(Top), DenseNet(Middle), EfficientNet(Bottom).

Table 1. Precison, Recall, F1-score, and AUC values for each model from the Kangnam dataset.

Dataset	Model	Classes	Precision	Recall	F1-score	AUC
Tagged	ResNet	Second	0.97	0.95	0.96	0.944
		Third	0.90	0.94	0.92	
	DenseNet	Second	1.00	0.96	0.98	0.981
		Third	0.93	1.00	0.96	
	EfficientNet	Second	0.99	0.97	0.98	0.977
		Third	0.94	0.99	0.96	
Original	ResNet	Second	0.99	0.92	0.96	0.955
		Third	0.87	0.99	0.92	
	DenseNet	Second	0.98	0.99	0.99	0.982
		Third	0.99	0.97	0.98	
	EfficientNet	Second	0.99	0.99	0.99	0.989
		Third	0.99	0.99	0.99	

when the model inferred the outcome. In the third-trimester period, it showed that the trend of the heatmap was focused on the fetal head. In contrast, it was highlighted around the internal os position or the space inside the internal os (lower uterus) on the mid-term period heatmap throughout. As a result, we found that the fetal head had an impact on the model. Additionally, the area including the internal os and lower uterus affected the model.

3.2 Difference in Heatmap with and Without Fetal Head

We compared which area is focused when the fetal head is or is not included in each class on ultrasound images. As depicted in Fig. 4., it showed that in

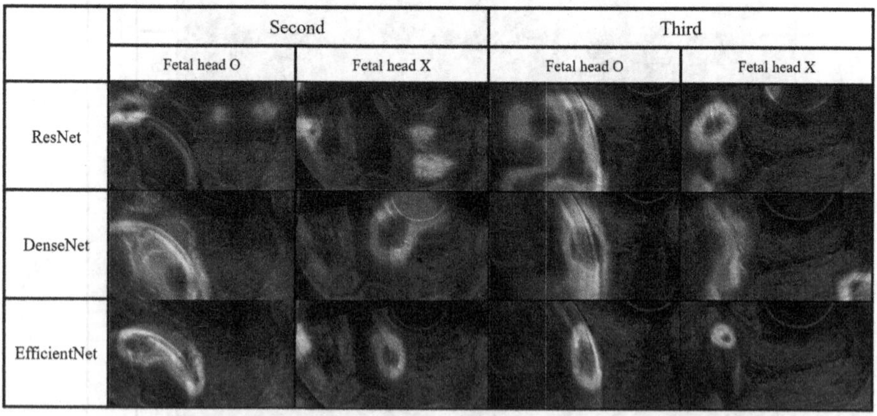

Fig. 4. The result of heatmaps using Grad-CAM++ for Second- and Third-trimester ultrasound images collected from the Kangnam dataset (original image) including fetal head or not.

Table 2. The performance of the model using test data collected from another institution.

Dataset	Model	Classes	Precision	Recall	F1-score	AUC
Tagged	ResNet	Second	0.81	0.97	0.88	0.904
		Third	0.97	0.84	0.90	
	DenseNet	Second	0.76	1.00	0.86	0.887
		Third	1.00	0.77	0.87	
	EfficientNet	Second	0.94	1.00	0.97	0.978
		Third	1.00	0.96	0.98	
Original	ResNet	Second	0.77	0.97	0.86	0.883
		Third	0.97	0.80	0.88	
	DenseNet	Second	0.77	0.93	0.84	0.982
		Third	0.94	0.80	0.86	
	EfficientNet	Second	0.90	0.96	0.93	0.94
		Third	0.97	0.92	0.95	

both classes, the heatmaps with fetal heads are highlighted according to the head. Whereas the results of the heatmap are emphasized around the internal os position of the cervix in middle-term images without fetal heads. Also in third-trimester images, it is highlighted lower uterus and cervix bolder. Through these results, we found that the internal os and lower uterus parts, in addition to the fetal head, had an effect on classifying second and third-trimester pregnancy.

3.3 Cross Validation Using Another Institution

External validation was conducted using data collected from another institution to generalize the model. We evaluated the test data collected from the Chungnam

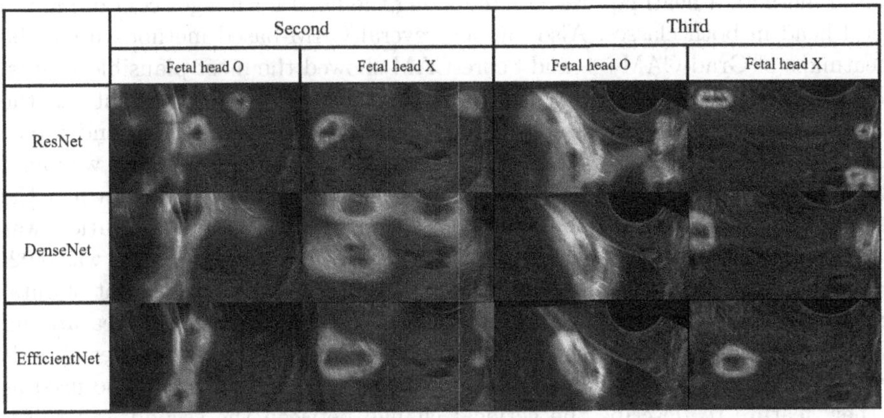

Fig. 5. The heatmap results were evaluated with the data collected from another institution for Second- and Third-trimester images (original image) with/without fetal head using Grad-CAM++.

National University Hospital with a pre-trained model with the Kangnam Sacred Hospital data. As a result, it showed a high AUC score in Table 2. Similar to the result evaluated with the Kangnam data, the image including the fetal head was highlighted along the head area in Fig. 5. Also, the heatmap images without the fetal head showed that it was highlighted around the internal os position.

4   Discussion and Conclusion

From the above CAM-based results, the fetal head appears to be the main factor that distinguishes second- and third-trimester images when a deep neural network is learning. The reason for these results is the fetal presentation [8]. As the third trimester draws near, the fetus moves through the positioning process in the womb for preparation shortly before birth. In this process, the baby twists, stretches, and goes down. It is repositioned mostly head-down toward the lower cervix, or internal os [9,14]. Therefore, in most of the third-trimester ultrasound images, they contained the fetal head. The part of the fetus's head included in the image seems to affect the model's learning. In particular, in the second trimester, when the fetal head was present, it was learned and classified according to the head. However, when there was no fetal head, it was found that the focus was on the internal os and lower uterus in EfficientNet. In DenseNet, it focused on the upper area of the cervical canal or anterior cervix area. These results shown by XAI methods might be used as a new feature to differentiate between second and third-trimester cervix.

In this paper, we trained a deep neural network for ultrasound imaging and compared the results of the model using eXplainable Artificial Intelligence (XAI) for identifying changes around the cervical canal area between second- and third-trimester pregnancy. The classification performance of the model showed an AUC of 0.96 on average. When the model's output was analyzed using a CAM-based method, a heatmap was created along the head for images containing the fetal head in both classes. Also, among several CAM-based methods used, the heatmaps of Grad-CAM++ and Score-CAM showed the most plausible results. This is because Score-CAM's heatmap appears to properly highlight via the process of identifying differences of importance for a given input, and Grad-CAM++ has good localization capabilities using gradients. Therefore, we found that the areas around the fetal head and internal os were affected when the model was trained. Additionally, data collected from another institution was used to test the model. The result showed that the average AUC score was 0.92. However, there are constraints on generalizing due to the small amount of data. So, we should collect more data and confirm whether there is an area around the cervical canal difference according to the second and third-trimester periods without the fetal head on the ultrasound images. This work might be used as a new feature to describe the cervical change between the second and third-trimester. In future work, it might be important evidence for studies affected by cervical changes, such as preterm birth.

Acknowledgment. This work was supported by the Korea Medical Device Development Fund grant funded by the Korea government (the Ministry of Science and ICT (MSIT), the Ministry of Trade, Industry and Energy, the Ministry of Health & Welfare, the Ministry of Food and Drug Safety) (No. 1711139109, KMDF_PR_20210527_0005) and partly supported by the Bio&Medical Technology Development Program of the National Research Foundation of Korea (NRF) grant funded by the Korean government (MSIT) (No. RS-2023-00223501).

References

1. Bach, S., Binder, A., Montavon, G., Klauschen, F., Müller, K.R., Samek, W.: On pixel-wise explanations for non-linear classifier decisions by layer-wise relevance propagation. PLoS ONE **10**(7), e0130140 (2015)
2. Chattopadhay, A., Sarkar, A., Howlader, P., Balasubramanian, V.N.: Gradcam++: Generalized gradient-based visual explanations for deep convolutional networks. In: 2018 IEEE Winter Conference on Applications of Computer Vision (WACV), pp. 839–847. IEEE (2018)
3. Cook, C.M., Ellwood, D.: A longitudinal study of the cervix in pregnancy using transvaginal ultrasound. BJOG: An International J. Obstetrics & Gynaecology **103**(1), 16–18 (1996)
4. Dagle, A.B., et al.: Automated segmentation of cervical anatomy to interrogate preterm birth. In: Licandro, R., Melbourne, A., Abaci Turk, E., Macgowan, C., Hutter, J. (eds.) Perinatal, Preterm and Paediatric Image Analysis: 7th International Workshop, PIPPI 2022, Held in Conjunction with MICCAI 2022, Singapore, September 18, 2022, Proceedings, pp. 48–59. Springer, Cham (2022). https://doi.org/10.1007/978-3-031-17117-8_5
5. García Ocaña, M.I., López-Linares Román, K., Burgos San Cristóbal, J., del Campo Real, A., Macía Oliver, I.: Prediction of failure of induction of labor from ultrasound images using radiomic features. In: Wang, Q., Gomez, A., Hutter, J., McLeod, K., Zimmer, V., Zettinig, O., Licandro, R., Robinson, E., Christiaens, D., Turk, E.A., Melbourne, A. (eds.) PIPPI/SUSI -2019. LNCS, vol. 11798, pp. 153–160. Springer, Cham (2019). https://doi.org/10.1007/978-3-030-32875-7_17
6. He, K., Zhang, X., Ren, S., Sun, J.: Deep residual learning for image recognition. In: Proceedings of the IEEE Conference on Computer Vision and Pattern Recognition, pp. 770–778 (2016)
7. Huang, G., Liu, Z., Van Der Maaten, L., Weinberger, K.Q.: Densely connected convolutional networks. In: Proceedings of the IEEE Conference on Computer Vision and Pattern Recognition, pp. 4700–4708 (2017)
8. Hughey, M.J.: Fetal position during pregnancy. Am. J. Obstet. Gynecol. **153**(8), 885–886 (1985)
9. Kilpatrick, S., Garrison, E.: Normal labor and delivery. Obstetrics: Normal Problem pregnancies **5**, 303–321 (2007)
10. Montavon, G., Lapuschkin, S., Binder, A., Samek, W., Müller, K.R.: Explaining nonlinear classification decisions with deep Taylor decomposition. Pattern Recogn. **65**, 211–222 (2017)
11. Muhammad, M.B., Yeasin, M.: Eigen-cam: Class activation map using principal components. In: 2020 International Joint Conference on Neural Networks (IJCNN), pp. 1–7. IEEE (2020)
12. Myers, K.M., et al.: The mechanical role of the cervix in pregnancy. J. Biomech. **48**(9), 1511–1523 (2015)

13. Nott, J.P., Bonney, E.A., Pickering, J.D., Simpson, N.A.: The structure and function of the cervix during pregnancy. Trans. Res. Anat. **2**, 1–7 (2016)
14. Popowski, T., Porcher, R., Fort, J., Javoise, S., Rozenberg, P.: Influence of ultrasound determination of fetal head position on mode of delivery: a pragmatic randomized trial (2015)
15. Selvaraju, R.R., Cogswell, M., Das, A., Vedantam, R., Parikh, D., Batra, D.: Gradcam: Visual explanations from deep networks via gradient-based localization. In: Proceedings of the IEEE International Conference on Computer Vision, pp. 618–626 (2017)
16. Son, G.H., You, Y.A., Kwon, E.J., Lee, K.Y., Kim, Y.J.: Comparative analysis of midtrimester amniotic fluid cytokine levels to predict spontaneous very preterm birth in patients with cervical insufficiency. Am. J. Reprod. Immunol. **75**(2), 155–161 (2016)
17. Spong, C.Y.: Prediction and prevention of recurrent spontaneous preterm birth. Obstet. Gynecol. **110**(2 Part 1), 405–415 (2007)
18. Spong, C.Y.: Defining "term" pregnancy: recommendations from the defining "term" pregnancy workgroup. JAMA **309**(23), 2445–2446 (2013)
19. Tan, M., Le, Q.: Efficientnet: Rethinking model scaling for convolutional neural networks. In: International Conference on Machine Learning, pp. 6105–6114. PMLR (2019)
20. Turek, M.: Explainable artificial intelligence (xai) (archived). https://www.darpa.mil/program/explainable-artificial-intelligence
21. Wang, H., et al.: Score-cam: Score-weighted visual explanations for convolutional neural networks. In: Proceedings of the IEEE/CVF Conference on Computer Vision and Pattern Recognition Workshops, pp. 24–25 (2020)
22. Włodarczyk, T., et al.: Estimation of preterm birth markers with u-net segmentation network. In: Wang, Q., et al. (eds.) PIPPI/SUSI -2019. LNCS, vol. 11798, pp. 95–103. Springer, Cham (2019). https://doi.org/10.1007/978-3-030-32875-7_11
23. Yost, N.P., et al.: Second-trimester cervical sonography: features other than cervical length to predict spontaneous preterm birth. Obstet. Gynecol. **103**(3), 457–462 (2004)
24. Zhou, B., Khosla, A., Lapedriza, A., Oliva, A., Torralba, A.: Learning deep features for discriminative localization. In: Proceedings of the IEEE Conference on Computer Vision and Pattern Recognition, pp. 2921–2929 (2016)

Infant Video Analysis

Automatic Infant Respiration Estimation from Video: A Deep Flow-Based Algorithm and a Novel Public Benchmark

Sai Kumar Reddy Manne[1,2], Shaotong Zhu[2], Sarah Ostadabbas[2],
and Michael Wan[1,2(✉)]

[1] Roux Institute, Northeastern University, Portland, ME, USA
mi.wan@northeastern.edu
[2] Augmented Cognition Lab, Department of Electrical and Computer Engineering,
Northeastern University, Boston, MA, USA

Abstract. Respiration is a critical vital sign for infants, and continuous respiratory monitoring is particularly important for newborns. However, neonates are sensitive and contact-based sensors present challenges in comfort, hygiene, and skin health, especially for preterm babies. As a step toward fully automatic, continuous, and contactless respiratory monitoring, we develop a deep-learning method for estimating respiratory rate and waveform from plain video footage in natural settings. Our automated infant respiration flow-based network (AIRFlowNet) combines video-extracted optical flow input and spatiotemporal convolutional processing tuned to the infant domain. We support our model with the first public annotated infant respiration dataset with 125 videos (AIR-125), drawn from eight infant subjects, set varied pose, lighting, and camera conditions. We include manual respiration annotations and optimize AIRFlowNet training on them using a novel spectral bandpass loss function. When trained and tested on the AIR-125 infant data, our method significantly outperforms other state-of-the-art methods in respiratory rate estimation, achieving a mean absolute error of ~2.9 breaths per minute, compared to ~4.7–6.2 for other public models designed for adult subjects and more uniform environments. (Our code and the manually annotated respiration (AIR-125) dataset can be found at https://github.com/ostadabbas/Infant-Respiration-Estimation. Supported by MathWorks and NSF-CAREER Grant #2143882.)

Keywords: Infant respiration measurement · Spatio-temporal neural network · Spectral loss · Vital sign monitoring

1 Introduction

From an infant's first breath in the seconds after birth, respiration becomes a critical vital sign in early life, with irregularities revealing complications ranging

D. Link-Sourani et al. (Eds.): PIPPI 2023, LNCS 14246, pp. 111–120, 2023.
https://doi.org/10.1007/978-3-031-45544-5_10

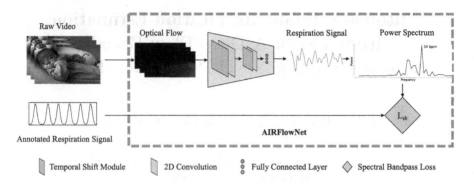

Fig. 1. Video-based respiration signal and rate estimation from our AIRFlowNet model trained with spectral bandpass loss and tested on our annotated infant respiration (AIR-125) dataset.

from apnea and respiratory distress in neonates [20], to respiratory syncytial virus (RSV) infection in months-old infants leading in severe cases to bronchiolitis or pneumonia [6], or even potentially to sudden infant death syndrome (SIDS) [23]. Continuous respiratory monitoring is particularly important for preterm infants during *ex utero* development in neonatal intensive care units (NICUs), where contactless sensors are desirable for comfort and hygiene, and to prevent skin damage, during this sensitive period [25]. We present a novel vision-based deep learning method for detecting an infant's respiration waveform and respiratory rate (see Fig. 1), as a step toward automated monitoring of infant breathing for both everyday and clinical diagnostic use. Only a few papers have explored deep learning-based infant respiration estimation (see Table 1), and due to logistical and privacy constraints on infant data collection, none of them publish their data or models and many draw data from just one or two infant subjects [4,11,18,24]. As part of this work, we publish the *annotated infant respiration dataset of 125 videos*, **AIR-125**, with ground truth respiratory rates and waveforms from eight infant subjects, to support public and reproducible research. AIR-125 features minute-long videos sourced from baby monitors and smartphone cameras in natural infant settings, with varying illumination, infant poses, age groups, and respiratory rates. We use manual respiration annotations rather than sensor-captured ground truth to enable data collection from various sources, but also include synthetically-generated respiration waveforms to maintain compatibility with existing models and benchmarks.

Existing approaches for respiration measurement [5,15] track motion using optical flow or track subtle color changes in skin pixels. The flow-based methods are prone to errors from noise or subject motion and the color-based methods rely on visible skin pixels in the video, which may be scarce for infants who are heavily covered or sleeping in an awkward pose like those in AIR-125. Hence, we also propose a new model, the *automated infant respiration flow-based network*, **AIRFlowNet**, which learns to isolate the periodic respiratory motion

Table 1. Datasets and methods in the literature for respiration estimation. PPG: Photoplethysmogram, PR: Pulse Rate, RR: Respiratory Rate, Resp: Respiration waveform, AU: Action Unit, BVP: Blood Volume Pulse, EEG: Electroencephalogram, ECG: Electrocardiogram, SpO2: Blood oxygenation, DL: Deep Learning, SP: Signal Processing.

Dataset	Ground Truth	Domain	Videos	Subjects	Public	Method
SCAMPS [19]	PPG, PR, RR, Resp, AU	Adult	2800	2800	✓	DL
COHFACE [7]	Resp, BVP	Adult	160	40	✓	SP
MAHNOB [22]	ECG, EEG, Resp	Adult	527	27	✓	None
AFRL [3]	ECG, EEG, PPG, PR, RR	Adult	300	25	✗	SP
OBF [12]	RR, PPG, ECG	Adult	212	106	✗	SP
Villarroel et al. [25]	Resp, PPG, SpO2	Infant	384	30	✗	DL
Földesy et al. [4]	Resp	Infant	1440	7	✗	DL
Kyrollos et al. [11]	Resp	Infant	20	1	✗	SP
Lorato et al. [18]	Resp	Infant	90	2	✗	SP
Tveit et al. [24]	RR	Infant	6	2	✗	SP
AIR-125 (ours)	Resp, RR, Pose	Infant	125	8	✓	DL

in a noisy environment without the need for visible skin in the video. Current respiration models are trained with ground truth obtained from contact sensors perfectly synchronized with videos [1,14,15]. We introduce a novel *spectral bandpass loss function* which encourages alignment in the frequency domain while forgiving absolute temporal shifts, enabling more effective training with our manual annotations. When trained and tested on AIR-125 infant data, AIR-FlowNet significantly outperforms other state-of-the-art respiration models.

In sum, our key contributions include (1) the first public annotated infant respiration dataset (AIR-125), (2) a motion-based infant respiration estimation model (AIRFlowNet) with a novel spectral bandpass loss achieving best-in-class performance, and (3) performance comparison of public color- and motion-based respiration models on infant and adult datasets.

2   Related Work

Respiration induces cyclical expansion and contraction in the chest and abdomen regions. Motion-based methods track this subtle motion in videos to estimate the respiration signal. Tveit *et al.* [24] use Rietz transform in a phase-based algorithm to track respiratory patterns and test their model on infant and adult subjects. Shao *et al.* [21] estimate both heart rate and breathing rate simultaneously by tracking shoulder motion and color changes in a subject's face. Guo *et al.* [5] improve the motion tracking using optical flow and human segmentation from pretrained deep learning models. Lorato *et al.* [18] use a two-stage approach to detect and reject video clips with severe motion, followed by a hand-crafted feature-based rate estimation. Kyrollos *et al.* [11] use depth information along with RGB videos to improve the accuracy. Földesy *et al.* [4] propose an incremental learning model to extract accurate frequency from a noisy estimate.

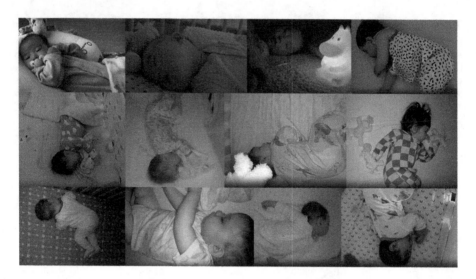

Fig. 2. Sample frames in our annotated infant respiration (AIR-125) dataset showing the diversity in pose, illumination, background, and camera type.

Another common approach for respiration estimation is based on the complex photoplethysmography (PPG) signal, a superposition of the slowly changing DC respiration component and the rapidly changing AC pulse component. Respiration waveform estimation based on color tracking was first introduced in DeepPhys [1]. Temporal shift modules were introduced in [14], in place of computationally expensive 3D convolutions, to improve efficiency of the model. Villarroel *et al.* [25] present a PPG signal extraction method for continuous infant monitoring in NICU setting. They use a multi-task CNN for segmenting skin pixels and detecting the presence of a subject in the camera, followed by simple pulse and breathing estimation. In [16], a few-shot adaptation of the base temporal shift deep learning model is used to improve results for individual subjects. In [27], a novel loss based on Pearson correlation is used to train the model, improving the estimation accuracy compared to a model trained with L^1 or L^2 losses. To the best of our knowledge, our work provides the first comparison study between color- and motion-based approaches for infant subjects, complementing the one existing study for adult subjects [26].

Finally, thermal imaging can be used to track the alternating cold and warm air flowing from the nose during inhalation and exhalation. Such methods [8,9,18] usually track a region of interest (ROI) in the nasal area across the video. Thermal cameras can be used in complete darkness, making them a good alternative to RGB cameras, but their setup cost prevents ubiquitous deployment.

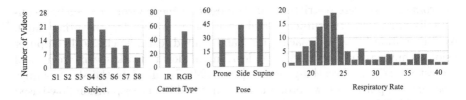

Fig. 3. Distribution of pose, camera type per subject, and respiratory rates (breaths per minute) in our annotated infant respiration (AIR-125) dataset.

3 AIR-125: An Annotated Infant Respiration Dataset

Available physiological measurement datasets are created synthetically [19] or extract reference physiological signals from contact-based systems and require the subjects situated in a controlled environment [7,25]. Unlike the existing datasets, AIR-125 features infant videos collected from a range of sources and settings to enable training and testing of flexible models useful for monitoring in everyday settings outside of the lab; our manual annotation process makes broad collection easier by eliminating equipment and recruitment constraints. Our primary source is baby monitor footage from five infants, captured during daylight and nighttime sleep sessions in-crib by our clinical team under Institutional Review Board (IRB #22-11-32) approval, with no other constraints on pose, lighting, clothing, and face visibility. The monitor switches between RGB and infrared (IR) modes depending on the light. For further diversity, we also source clips from three infant subjects on YouTube. From both sources, we extract a combined dataset of 125 videos, each approximately 60 s long. For respiration annotations, we parse through video frames, focusing on thoracic or abdominal motion to determine start times of exhalation cycles aided by the VGG Image Annotator [2]. Annotated respiratory rates range from 18–42 breaths per minute; see Fig. 3 for distributions by subject, pose, camera type, and respiratory rate.

The annotations from each video clip are converted to an impulse sequence, with one pulse per exhalation start time label. To create smooth waveforms that are analogous to signals from a contact-based respiration system, the impulse sequence is Gaussian filtered with an empirically determined radius of 4 frames. The smoothed waveform is used as ground truth signal for our respiratory rate estimation methods. The video resolutions range from 854×480 to 1920×1080 and frame rates from 10–30 Hz.

4 Methodology

4.1 AirFlowNet Architecture

Color-based approaches track imperceptible color changes to estimate the remote photoplethysmography (rPPG) signal and isolate the breathing signal from a complex superposition of other vital signals [1]. Hence, these methods are prone to errors unless severe restrictions are imposed on the environment such as constant illumination, still subjects, and no camera motion. On the other hand, existing motion-based approaches use hand-crafted features, classical computer vision techniques, or pretrained deep learning models to track specific regions of interest to estimate breathing signals [10,21,24]. To alleviate the shortcomings of these two approaches, we propose our annotated infant respiration flow-based network (AIRFlowNet), depicted in Fig. 1, which processes optical flow input with a spatio-temporal convolutional network and isolates a clean respiration signal from a noisy video with possible subject or camera motion. Using optical flow input also eliminates the need to retrain a model when testing on videos from different camera types such as RGB and IR cameras, consequently improving generalizablity across various datasets.

We use a simple yet accurate implementation of coarse-to-fine optical flow [13] for our experiments. The optical flow is generated at 96×96 resolution to preserve the subtle motion induced by respiration and reduce the effects of spatial noise in the flow calculation. The calculated flow vectors are stored in HSV color space at a frame rate of 5 Hz.

We base our convolutional network on EfficientPhys [15], adapting it to optical flow inputs. We replace the difference layer in EfficientPhys with a convolution layer followed by a batch-normalization layer as our inputs are Z-score normalized in the preprocessing stage. The first convolution layer follows a series of temporal shift modules [14] and convolution layers that efficiently compute temporal features by shifting the channels across time dimension. Self-attention blocks following the temporal shift modules refine the features to appropriately weigh different spatial locations that correspond to respiration motion. A dense layer is used at the end of the network to estimate a 1D respiration signal. Unlike EfficientPhys, which estimates the first order derivative of the signal, our model estimates the respiration signal directly.

4.2 Spectral Bandpass Loss

Current respiration estimation models train the networks using the L^2 loss between the ground truth signal and the predicted respiration waveform. While L^2 loss is useful for training with a ground truth signal that is precisely synchronized with the video, such as that obtained from electronic sensors, any temporal misalignment can lead to erroneous results. Since our manual annotations do not enjoy near-perfect alignment, we employ a new loss function that imposes a penalty entirely in the frequency domain, to prevent slight temporal misalignments from impeding effective learning of respiratory rate.

For any waveform $x = x(t)$, we use the fast Fourier transform $\mathcal{F}$ to define its corresponding power spectral density $X_{\mathrm{PSD}} := |\mathcal{F}(x - x_0)|^2$, where x_0 is the temporal mean of x. After computing power spectral densities Y_{PSD} and $\hat{Y}_{\mathrm{PSD}}$ for the predicted (y) and the reference waveform $(\hat{y})$ respectively, we filter out the power from frequencies outside the normal infant breathing range of 0.3–1.0 Hz using a bandpass filter, $B(\cdot)$. The filtered power spectral densities are normalized to have a unit cumulative power. We define the **spectral bandpass loss** L_{sb} between y and $\hat{y}$ by

$$L_{sb}(y, \hat{y}) = \left\| \frac{B(Y_{PSD})}{\sum_{\xi \in \Xi} B(Y_{PSD})} - \frac{B(\hat{Y}_{PSD})}{\sum_{\xi \in \Xi} B(\hat{Y}_{PSD})} \right\|_2, \qquad (1)$$

with the outer norm being the L^2 norm, and Ξ constituting the set of frequencies in the power spectrum.

5   Evaluation and Results

5.1   Experimental Setup

Datasets. We evaluate our model on a public adult dataset, COHFACE [7], along with our infant dataset. COHFACE contains 160 webcam clips from 40 subjects, each approximately 60 s long. The videos are recorded at 640×480 resolution and 20 Hz, under both ambient and normal lighting conditions. Reference respiration signals come from a respiration belt readout at 32 Hz.

Training. To train and evaluate our models on COHFACE, we use the rPPG-toolbox [17], which provides a training framework for several physiological signal estimation models designed for adult subjects. We use the toolbox to train current state-of-the-art physiological measurement models: DeepPhys [1], TS-CAN [14], and EfficientPhys [15]. For the color-based model training, the dataset is preprocessed to detect a face in each frame using Haar cascade classifier. The frames are then cropped around the face bounding box, and resized to a lower resolution of 96×96. All the models are trained with L^2 loss to generate a continuous signal for each clip. To train AIRFlowNet, we estimate the optical flow for each video and do not perform any face-based preprocessing. The rest of the training methodology is identical between all the trained models.

Post-processing. The estimated respiration signals are first filtered using a bandpass filter to remove noise from external sources. The lower and upper cut-off frequencies for the bandpass filter are 0.3 Hz and 1.0 Hz, covering the normal infant respiratory rates of 18–60 breaths per minute. The filtered signal is then transformed to frequency domain through a fast Fourier transform. We perform power spectral density analysis to determine the frequency with the maximal power as the predicted respiratory rate. We calculate three metrics that are commonly used in the literature to compare the different approaches: mean absolute error (MAE), root mean squared error (RMSE), and Pearson's correlation coefficient (ρ).

5.2   Results and Analysis

We tabulate results from the following three experimental configurations (training dataset → testing dataset) in Table 2.

Table 2. Comparison of different motion-based (†) and color-based (⋆) methods under various train → test data configurations (COHFACE for adult, AIR-125 for infant). Note that [5] does not learn from respiration data.

Method	Adult → Adult			Adult → Infant			Infant → Infant		
	MAE ↓ (bpm)	RMSE ↓ (bpm)	ρ ↑	MAE ↓ (bpm)	RMSE ↓ (bpm)	ρ ↑	MAE ↓ (bpm)	RMSE ↓ (bpm)	ρ ↑
Eff-Phys⋆ [15]	4.07	5.46	0.27	7.21	9.08	0.40	6.22	7.83	0.44
DeepPhys⋆ [1]	2.68	4.64	0.36	6.76	9.29	0.38	6.06	8.79	0.38
TS-CAN⋆ [14]	2.25	3.96	0.53	8.84	11.6	0.20	6.35	7.54	0.50
Guo et al.† [5]	1.04	2.45	**0.82**	4.68	6.74	0.32	4.68	6.74	0.32
AIRFlowNet†	**1.01**	**2.20**	0.76	**4.16**	**5.98**	**0.41**	**2.91**	**5.40**	**0.72**

Table 3. AIRFlowNet performance when trained and tested on AIR-125 data using common loss functions and our novel spectral bandpass loss L_{sb}.

Metric		L^1	L^2	$-\rho$	L_{sb} (ours)
MAE	↓	3.49	3.46	2.96	**2.91**
RMSE	↓	6.26	5.36	**5.34**	5.40
ρ	↑	0.64	0.70	0.71	**0.72**

Adult → Adult. We compare our model with color-based methods [1,14,15] trained on COHFACE and the motion-based method from [5]. Since COHFACE has very still subjects with no external motion, motion-based approaches perform better than color-based models.

Adult → Infant. We quantify the domain generalizability of all approaches by training on COHFACE and testing on AIR-125. The AIR-125 dataset is divided into train and test splits, with 50 clips from 3 subjects in the training split, and 75 videos from the remaining 5 subjects in the test split. Our model demonstrates better generalizability as it is agnostic to camera type and brightness changes owing to the optical flow input.

Infant → Infant. For a fair comparison, we train and test both AIRFlowNet and the other models designed for adult subjects purely on AIR-125 data. Even when trained on infant data, the other models struggle to attain acceptable performance, exhibiting high mean absolute error and low Pearson's correlation. Our model achieves the best infant-domain performance, and the quantitative results even rival the performances of adult models tested on adult data.

Ablation Study. To demonstrate the effectiveness of our spectral bandpass loss L_{sb}, we compare results of AIRFlowNet trained and tested on AIR-125 data under L_{sb} and three other common loss functions—L^1, L^2, and negative Pearson loss $(-\rho)$ [27]—in Table 3. The L_{sb} loss performs best, but $-\rho$ is also effective, likely because it also relaxes constraints on strictly matching the ground-truth signal, compared to the L^1 and L^2 losses. Note, however, that training with $-\rho$ requires ground truth waveforms (synthetically generated in AIR-125), whereas L_{sb} can be trained with respiration exhalation timestamps alone.

As AIRFlowNet is based on an efficient model from [15], processing a 96×96 frame takes 4.16 ms on a V100 GPU. However, the optical flow computation [13] requires 162 ms and poses a challenge in realtime monitoring.

6 Conclusion

We have presented the first public annotated infant respiration dataset, AIR-125, together with a novel deep learning model, AIRFlowNet, tuned for infant subjects and achieving state-of-the-art performance on AIR-125. Our model uses optical flow, spatio-temporal learning, and a new spectral bandpass loss function to optimize performance across varied lighting and camera settings, toward the eventual goal of automated, continuous, and purely video-based infant respiratory monitoring, both in NICU and at-home settings. Fruitful work in the future could include expanding the dataset scope and model performance, or achieving similar performance without using dense optical flow to enable immediate real-time monitoring in critical care situations.

References

1. Chen, W., McDuff, D.: Deepphys: Video-based physiological measurement using convolutional attention networks. In: Proceedings of the European Conference on Computer Vision (ECCV), pp. 349–365 (2018)
2. Dutta, A., Zisserman, A.: The VIA annotation software for images, audio and video. In: Proceedings of the 27th ACM International Conference on Multimedia. MM '19, ACM, New York, NY, USA (2019). https://doi.org/10.1145/3343031.3350535
3. Estepp, J.R., Blackford, E.B., Meier, C.M.: Recovering pulse rate during motion artifact with a multi-imager array for non-contact imaging photoplethysmography. In: 2014 IEEE International Conference on Systems, Man, and Cybernetics (SMC), pp. 1462–1469. IEEE (2014)
4. Földesy, P., Zarándy, Á., Szabó, M.: Reference free incremental deep learning model applied for camera-based respiration monitoring. IEEE Sens. J. **21**(2), 2346–2352 (2020)
5. Guo, T., Lin, Q., Allebach, J.: Remote estimation of respiration rate by optical flow using convolutional neural networks. Electron. Imaging **2021**(8), 1–267 (2021)
6. Hall, C.B., et al.: The burden of respiratory syncytial virus infection in young children. N. Engl. J. Med. **360**(6), 588–598 (2009)
7. Heusch, G., Anjos, A., Marcel, S.: A reproducible study on remote heart rate measurement. arXiv preprint arXiv:1709.00962 (2017)
8. Hochhausen, N., Barbosa Pereira, C., Leonhardt, S., Rossaint, R., Czaplik, M.: Estimating respiratory rate in post-anesthesia care unit patients using infrared thermography: an observational study. Sensors **18**(5), 1618 (2018)

9. Jakkaew, P., Onoye, T.: Non-contact respiration monitoring and body movements detection for sleep using thermal imaging. Sensors **20**(21), 6307 (2020)
10. Koolen, N., et al.: Automated respiration detection from neonatal video data. In: ICPRAM (2), pp. 164–169 (2015)
11. Kyrollos, D.G., Tanner, J.B., Greenwood, K., Harrold, J., Green, J.R.: Noncontact neonatal respiration rate estimation using machine vision. In: 2021 IEEE Sensors Applications Symposium (SAS), pp. 1–6. IEEE (2021)
12. Li, X., et al.: The obf database: A large face video database for remote physiological signal measurement and atrial fibrillation detection. In: 2018 13th IEEE International Conference on Automatic Face Gesture Recognition (FG 2018), pp. 242–249. IEEE (2018)
13. Liu, C., et al.: Beyond pixels: exploring new representations and applications for motion analysis. Ph.D. thesis, Massachusetts Institute of Technology (2009)
14. Liu, X., Fromm, J., Patel, S., McDuff, D.: Multi-task temporal shift attention networks for on-device contactless vitals measurement. Adv. Neural. Inf. Process. Syst. **33**, 19400–19411 (2020)
15. Liu, X., Hill, B., Jiang, Z., Patel, S., McDuff, D.: Efficientphys: Enabling simple, fast and accurate camera-based cardiac measurement. In: Proceedings of the IEEE/CVF Winter Conference on Applications of Computer Vision, pp. 5008–5017 (2023)
16. Liu, X., Jiang, Z., Fromm, J., Xu, X., Patel, S., McDuff, D.: Metaphys: few-shot adaptation for non-contact physiological measurement. In: Proceedings of the Conference on Health, Inference, and Learning. pp. 154–163 (2021)
17. Liu, X., et al.: Deep physiological sensing toolbox. arXiv preprint arXiv:2210.00716 (2022)
18. Lorato, I., et al.: Towards continuous camera-based respiration monitoring in infants. Sensors **21**(7), 2268 (2021)
19. McDuff, D., et al.: Scamps: synthetics for camera measurement of physiological signals. Adv. Neural. Inf. Process. Syst. **35**, 3744–3757 (2022)
20. Reuter, S., Moser, C., Baack, M.: Respiratory distress in the newborn. Pediatr. Rev. **35**(10), 417–429 (10 2014)
21. Shao, D., Yang, Y., Liu, C., Tsow, F., Yu, H., Tao, N.: Noncontact monitoring breathing pattern, exhalation flow rate and pulse transit time. IEEE Trans. Biomed. Eng. **61**(11), 2760–2767 (2014)
22. Soleymani, M., Lichtenauer, J., Pun, T., Pantic, M.: A multimodal database for affect recognition and implicit tagging. IEEE Trans. Affect. Comput. **3**(1), 42–55 (2011)
23. Thach, B.T.: The role of respiratory control disorders in SIDS. Respir. Physiol. Neurobiol. **149**(1), 343–353 (2005), dev. of Respiratory Control
24. Tveit, D.M., Engan, K., Austvoll, I., Meinich-Bache, Ø.: Motion based detection of respiration rate in infants using video. In: 2016 IEEE International Conference on Image Processing (ICIP), pp. 1225–1229. IEEE (2016)
25. Villarroel, M., et al.: Non-contact physiological monitoring of preterm infants in the Neonatal Intensive Care Unit. NPJ Digital Med. **2**(1), 128 (2019)
26. Wang, W., den Brinker, A.C.: Camera-based respiration monitoring: Motion and PPG-based measurement. In: Contactless Vital Signs Monitoring, pp. 79–97. Elsevier (2022)
27. Yu, Z., Li, X., Zhao, G.: Remote photoplethysmograph signal measurement from facial videos using spatio-temporal networks. arXiv preprint arXiv:1905.02419 (2019)

Author Index

D. Link-Sourani et al. (Eds.): PIPPI 2023, LNCS 14246, pp. 121–122, 2023.
https://doi.org/10.1007/978-3-031-45544-5

Printed in the United States
by Baker & Taylor Publisher Services